GORDON RUSSELL

Designer of Furniture

GORDON RUSSELL

Designer of Furniture

1892–1992

Jeremy Myerson

Published for the centenary of Gordon Russell's birth
by the Design Council/Gordon Russell Limited

Published in the United Kingdom by
The Design Council
28 Haymarket
London SW1Y 4SU
for Gordon Russell Limited
in association with the Gordon Russell Trust
High Street
Broadway
Worcestershire WR12 7AD

Printed and bound in United Kingdom by
Butler & Tanner Ltd
Frome, Somerset

Designed by Nicole Griffin

British Library Cataloguing in Publication Data
A catalogue record for this book is available from the British Library

ISBN 0 85072 306 X

ILLUSTRATION ACKNOWLEDGEMENTS
Illustrations in this book are reproduced with the permission of those listed below. The copyright of illustrations not listed here is held by Gordon Russell Limited. Ian Dobbie: pages 32, 33, 56, 57, 62 bottom, 82, 83; Marian Pepler: page 66 top and bottom, page 69 top; The Controller of Her Majesty's Stationery Office: pages 84, 85, 86, 87 (with thanks to the Geffrye Museum); Victoria and Albert Museum: page 88; Lady Reilly: page 98; The Design Council: page 27, 46 bottom, 99, 102 top and bottom, 121 top and bottom, 122; Ray Leigh: page 115

Contents page illustration: Russell Workshops logo dating from the late 1920s

Author's acknowledgements

This book would not have been possible without the active involvement of my two collaborators, Ray Leigh and Trevor Chinn. Both knew Sir Gordon Russell well personally and both played a key role in the professional development of his company. Their historical knowledge, psychological insights and practical support proved invaluable.

I would also like to thank the following people for their recollections and contributions: Kate Baynes, Sir Terence Conran, Douglas Barrington, L J Smith, Val Freeman, Bill Ould, Marian Pepler, Ken Baynes, Sir Geoffrey Jellicoe, Alison Garfield, Dan Johnston, Keith Grant, Kirk Ritchie, Tibor Reich, Edward Cory, Mino Vernaschi, Adrian Stokes and Gerard Taylor.

My special thanks to my editor Suzie Duke and designer Nicole Griffin at the Design Council for their sterling work; to Wendy Smith for her comments on the draft manuscript; and, lastly, to Matthew and Nathan Myerson for their patience in allowing me to get the job done.

Jeremy Myerson

Jeremy Myerson is a leading writer on twentieth-century design. His books include the Conran Design Guides to *Tableware, Kitchenware, Lamps and Lighting* and the *Home Office*. A former editor of *Creative Review* and assistant editor of *Design*, he founded the world's first news magazine for designers, *Design Week*, in 1986. His work has appeared in numerous newspapers and magazines, including *The Times, Financial Times, The Guardian* and *The Daily Telegraph*.

Contents

INTRODUCTION *by* RAY LEIGH

For Gordon Russell to describe himself as a 'Designer of Furniture' in his army record book of 1917 was boldly prophetic, particularly since his chances of living through the horror of the First World War to fulfil his ambition were next to nothing. In his autobiography, *Designer's Trade,* he expressed his belief that every era should build on the achievements of the past: 'To me it was a poor age which could make no contribution of its own'. This feeling was to provide the motivation for all that Gordon himself achieved in the future.

Gordon Russell's crusading career and the success of Gordon Russell Ltd show a remarkable dedication to design and quality. To sustain such commitment through the ups and downs of the furniture industry requires special qualities – determination, the ability to respond to new market opportunities and, above all, the ability to lead, motivate and inspire. That Gordon Russell had these qualities in abundance is eminently clear from the recollections of those who knew him.

I first met Gordon in the early 1950s at the time of the Festival of Britain, when, during a vacation from study at the Architectural Association, I worked as a very junior assistant in the offices of Dick Russell and Robert Goodden. They were busy designing the Lion and Unicorn building for the Festival. After the austerity of the war years it was an exciting and heady period. I little thought at the time that for the next 40 years I would have the good fortune to become totally involved with the Russell family and their various enterprises.

I subsequently joined Dick's practice, and he, Ian Hodgson and I eventually formed a partnership which continued until 1967. It was during this period that I came to know Gordon well, as the practice was continuously engaged in alterations to the family-owned Lygon Arms (run by the third brother, Don, with Douglas Barrington), and in the completion of Gordon's home at Kingcombe.

Working for all three brothers brought home to me the passion for quality and excellence which they shared. It was impossible not to be infected by their commitment to high standards and attention to detail. Gordon and Dick were impressive figures: Gordon, a big man in all respects, physically strong and vigorous; Dick, tall and elegant, now recognized as one of the country's leading designers. At the Lygon Arms, Don, with his constant attention to the comfort of his guests, epitomized the very best qualities of 'mine host'.

I joined Gordon Russell Ltd in 1967. Although from 1940 Gordon held no more executive directorships with the company, his influence in 1967 was still powerful. His belief in training and his ability to command loyalty assured us of a superb and stable workforce, many of whom had known Gordon since the early days. In 1968 when he gave me a copy of his autobiography, he added the inscription, 'To Ray, an enthusiastic new boy in this adventure'. Although we were serious about our objectives, it certainly was a great adventure: a stream of new designs flowing from the company, the involvement of outside consultant designers, overseas initiatives in the Middle East, Europe and Japan. In all these activities Gordon was entirely supportive and continued to play his part in meeting and entertaining many of the distinguished visitors to Broadway. After the death of Don in 1970, Gordon was appointed chairman of the company. In 1971 I succeeded Bill Ould as managing director and thereafter enjoyed the most marvellous association with Gordon up to his death.

Although when I joined the company I was aware of Gordon's impressive record as a designer, nothing had quite prepared me for the revelation that presented itself when I came to look at the archives. In just ten years, between 1920 and 1930, he produced hundreds of designs not only for furniture but also for metalwork and glassware – a prolific output of quality from a man who had never received any formal design training. The range of Gordon's interests and skills was extraordinary. They included carving and lettering: in 1939, for example, he carved a 16-foot inscription in stone for Dovers House in Chipping Campden, the home of Fred Griggs, artist and engraver, and one of the last Arts and Crafts houses built in England.

I am sure that all of Gordon's happiest moments were spent in his garden at Kingcombe, which for over 50 years he planned and constructed with his own hands. His stone walls and terracing were superb, and on a scale which few of us would contemplate even starting – though he recommended it as a great way to lose oneself for hours. When replacing a section of dry stonewalling myself, I often remember him at well over 75 manoeuvering and lifting immense pieces of stone.

Gordon always enjoyed telling a good story against himself, such as his account of obtaining a large stone for the head of steps at the entrance to Kingcombe. Having spotted the ideal stone in a nearby field owned by a local farmer, he deliberated on how best to approach the man. Deciding on practical, down-to-earth tactics he suggested to him that it must have obstructed ploughing and grass-cutting for years, and offered to remove it as a favour. To Gordon's surprise, this 'simple fellow' replied that despite the inconvenience he had come to love the stone and would miss it, but sensing Gordon's disappointment offered him a choice from a nearby quarry.

After a day in Broadway at the workshops I would often call in on Gordon to discuss over a bottle of wine all that was happening. He continued to the end of his life to take a keen interest in the company, always offering advice and giving support. Invariably on a fine summer evening we would wander through the garden, as Gordon explained the latest project and outlined his long-term plans. Today Kingcombe stands as a testimony to his vision and concern for fine building and the English landscape.

Gordon's wife, Toni, would say to me: 'Of course he thinks he is immortal – he will have to live forever to complete all that he is planning'. One of those plans was the creation of the public garden in Chipping Campden in memory of the Campden-born plant-hunter Ernest Wilson. Thanks to Gordon's initiative, the site was saved from development and, though sadly completed only after Gordon's death, stands not only as a tribute to both men but as a symbol of Gordon's love and concern for Campden.

Above all Gordon Russell was a realist who well understood and also impressed on us that if a company was to survive and prosper and stick to its principles, it must respond to new market challenges and sometimes change direction. This is as true today as at any time in the last 70 years and the company's continued commitment to the highest standards of design and quality are still as strong as ever.

Gordon Russell believed passionately that every age must make a contribution of its own and he dedicated his life to uniting design and industry. Another great design crusader, Sir Terence Conran, has recently remarked: 'The sedentary life is not for me. I hope I die with an unfulfilled project on the go.' They might have been Gordon's own words – they certainly typified his life.

Ray Leigh
January 1992

Chronology

SIR GORDON RUSSELL

1892 Born in Cricklewood, London, 20 May

1904 Moves with the family to Broadway, Worcestershire

1908 Joins the family business after leaving Chipping Campden Grammar School

1914 Signs up with the Worcestershire Regiment to fight in World War One

1917 Describes himself as 'Designer of Furniture' in officer's record book

1919 Rejoins the family business after demobilization

1921 Marries Toni Denning

1922 Holds first exhibition of own designs at Cheltenham

1923 Publishes manifesto for modern design, *Honesty and The Crafts*

1925 Initiates building work on the family home at Kingcombe

1926 Joins Art Workers' Guild

1927 Arranges for younger brother Dick to train as an architect at the Architectural Association in London

1928 One-man show at the Arlington Gallery, Bond Street, London

1930 Terminates designing activities

1933 Takes over from his father as managing director of the furniture firm

1936 Extension added to Kingcombe

1938 Father, S B Russell, dies

1940 Forced to resign from executive control of the furniture company. Elected Royal Designer for Industry

1942 Invited to join the Utility Furniture Advisory Committee

1943 Appointed chairman of the Utility Furniture Design Panel

1944 Becomes founder member of the newly constituted Council of Industrial Design

1945 Takes a leading role in the organization of the 'Britain Can Make It' exhibition

1947 Awarded CBE. Appointed Director of the Council of Industrial Design

1949 Oversees the launch of the COID's *Design* magazine

1951 Plays a major part in the organization of the Festival of Britain

1955 Knighted in the New Year's Honours List

1956 Responsible for the opening of the COID's Design Centre at 28 Haymarket, London. Mother dies

1959 Appointed Senior Fellow of the Royal College of Art. Retires from post of Director of the COID

1960 Sets up consultancy at Kingcombe

1962 Appointed Master of the Art Workers' Guild, and awarded the RSA Gold Medal for services to industrial design

1964 *Looking at Furniture* published by Lund Humphries

1968 Autobiography *Designer's Trade* published by George Allen & Unwin. Death of youngest son, Oliver John.

1970 Death of elder brother, Don

1977 After a gap of 47 years starts designing again, in collaboration with Adriaan Hermsen

1978 Gives 'Skill' address to the Faculty of Royal Designers for Industry at the Royal Society of Arts

1980 Presented with an Honorary Doctorate by the Royal College of Art. Dies at Kingcombe. Buried at Chipping Campden

1992 Centenary of his birth commemorated with an exhibition and the publication of this book

GORDON RUSSELL FURNITURE

1904 Gordon Russell's father, S B Russell, buys the Lygon Arms hotel in Broadway

1919 Family business, including furniture repair workshops, renamed Russell & Sons

1920 Lygon Cottage acquired as showroom

1923 Company receives first order – an entire dining-room for Albert Hartley – and shows model café alongside Heal's room at Victoria and Albert Museum exhibition

1925 Russell & Sons wins gold award at Paris Exhibition for a walnut cabinet

1927 Company renamed The Russell Workshops

1929 Company renamed Gordon Russell Ltd and opens London showroom at 28 Wigmore Street. Dick Russell appointed head of the drawing office at the Broadway factory

1931 Gordon Russell Ltd begins to design and manufacture radio cabinets for Murphy

1933 Marian Pepler becomes buyer of factored goods for the company

1934 W H 'Curly' Russell is appointed chief designer at Broadway

1935 Factory is opened in Park Royal, London; new showroom opened at 40 Wigmore Street

1936 Nikolaus Pevsner becomes chief buyer

1937 Company shows room set designed by Curly Russell and Marian Pepler at Paris International Exhibition

1939 Royal Warrant granted by Queen Elizabeth (the Queen Mother). Staff magazine *The Circular Saw* published for the first time

1940 R H Bee becomes managing director. The London showroom is closed down and the Broadway factory turned over to war work

1941 Park Royal factory closed down

1943 Company joins Utility Furniture programme

1946 Gordon Russell Ltd exhibits at 'Britain Can Make It', and expands into the retail market. The Russell Furnishings contract company is established

1950 Ted Ould takes over from R H Bee as managing director

1957 Presentation table produced as a gift to President Eisenhower from the Queen

1960 Chairs produced for Coventry Cathedral to a design by Dick Russell

1961 Royal Warrant granted by Queen Elizabeth II

1966 Bill Ould succeeds brother Ted as managing director

1967 Ray Leigh appointed design director

1968 Official visit by Duke of Edinburgh to Broadway

1969 Trevor Chinn replaces Curly Russell as chief designer

1970 Gordon Russell Ltd withdraws from retail market to concentrate on contract work

1971 Ray Leigh is appointed managing director. The company pursues a policy of design-led international expansion

1979 Company wins RSA Presidential Award for Design Management

1982 Ray Leigh becomes chairman. Chris Whittard and Laurie Wolder are appointed joint managing directors

1984 International design competition organized in association with *Architectural Review* and the Design Council

1986 Giroflex acquires the company, renamed Gordon Russell plc to spearhead the launch of the furniture group onto the London Stock Exchange

1989 Gordon Russell plc is acquired by Steelcase Strafor

1992 A new executive desking range designed by Gerard Taylor and Daniel Weil is launched to coincide with the centenary of the company's founder

Chapter 1

1892–1918

EARLY INFLUENCES *in* THE COTSWOLDS

Gordon Russell stands as a towering figure in British twentieth-century design. Yet all the depth of his experience, the breadth of his achievements, and the substance of his international reputation can be traced back to a single place – Broadway in Worcestershire, a jewel of a village hidden in the Cotswold Hills. It is both ironic and wholly appropriate that Gordon Russell's influence over the course of modern British design as designer and manufacturer, administrator and educationalist, writer and thinker should have its roots, not in one of Britain's large, mechanized, desensitized industrial cities, but in this beautifully proportioned village with its well-mannered architecture and traditional quality scarcely touched by the passing of time, despite the growing volume of tourists and traffic.

Broadway at the end of the twentieth century is certainly a busier place than the one which greeted Gordon Russell and his family when they first arrived in 1904, but it nevertheless retains the same air of unpretentious, honest charm which so informed his early designs. The village can claim two quintessentially English institutions, both of them put on the map by the Russell family: one, the Lygon Arms, flaunts its grandness on the broad main street and is without doubt one of Britain's finest country hotels; the other, Gordon Russell Furniture, is scarcely visible and yet one of Britain's most famous furniture factories.

This page and opposite: the Lygon Arms, Broadway, purchased by Gordon Russell's father in 1904. The grand country hotel exerted a strong aesthetic influence on Gordon Russell in his early years

9

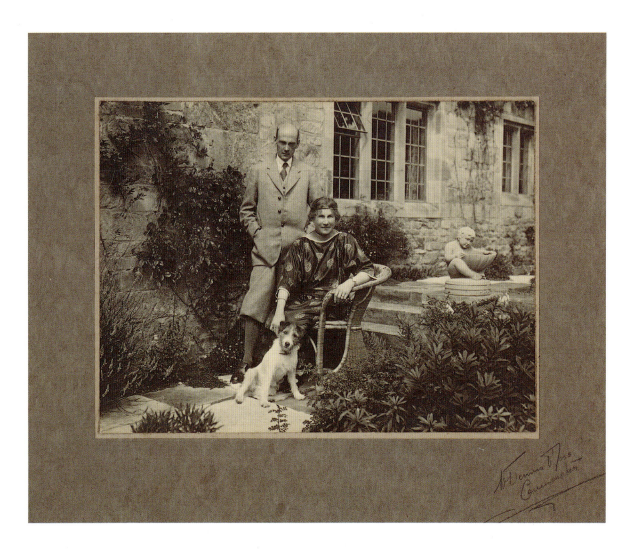

Above: Gordon Russell's parents. Single-minded and pioneering, they became well-known figures in the local community. Right: the family in Broadway, with youngest son Dick still a baby

The interrelationship between the hotel and the furniture company, and the influence of the Broadway environment, resound as keynotes throughout Gordon Russell's life and work, but Gordon did not set eyes on the village until the age of 12. He was born on 20 May 1892, the second year of his parents' marriage, in a small, semi-rural cottage in Cricklewood, London. His father, Sydney Bolton Russell, was a clerk in the Knightsbridge branch of the London and County Bank on a salary of around £150 a year. His mother, Elizabeth Shefford, was from a Windsor farming family with whom she swiftly lost contact. The father in particular was to prove a formidable influence on his eldest son's development as a designer and entrepreneur.

There were three Russell boys: Gordon (Sydney Gordon), Don (Donald George Shefford, born in 1894) and Dick (Richard Drew, born in 1903). All of them were destined to excel in different branches of the family business. In his autobiography, *Designer's Trade*, Gordon recalled living as a young child in a 'smart, hard, ugly and monotonous little suburban house' on Tooting Bec Road in south London. It was, he explained, 'like thousands of older houses which, year by year, ate up the countryside around London. No slightest hint of the emotions which building had once stirred in the breasts of men obtruded itself anywhere.' These were emotions which Gordon Russell would experience only when the family had moved to Broadway.

In 1901 S B Russell took a job as an agency manager with a firm of brewers in Burton-on-Trent, Samuel Allsopp & Sons. The family moved to a cottage in the Derbyshire village of Repton. 'To a highly strung boy coming from the noise and bustle of London,' wrote Gordon Russell in his autobiography, 'the quietness and slower tempo of the country were most soothing.' His father had to travel widely around the area visiting the country inns and public houses for which he was now responsible. One of these properties was the Lygon Arms at Broadway. The place caught his imagination and he wrote to his employers urging them to develop the 'splendid piece of Cotswolds architecture' as a country hotel, not as a hostelry for beer sales. The brewery was not interested.

In an extraordinary move S B Russell decided to buy the Lygon Arms himself and go into the hotel business, without any previous experience of innkeeping or catering. His father had managed the Cotton Estate in Mile End and S B Russell himself had considerable experience of managing a business, but the Lygon Arms in its run-down state was an entirely different venture which demanded an entirely new set of skills from the former bank clerk and his young sons. The success with which the Russells went on to restore the old hotel and build its popularity is proof of the family's single-mindedness in the pursuit of quality.

To purchase the Lygon Arms – the sum was believed to be about £4,000 – S B Russell borrowed money from R C Drew, a London businessman with hotel interests whose books he had kept while working for the bank. It was in gratitude

The Lygon Arms hotel on
Broadway's wide main street.
S B Russell foresaw that the
motor car would open up
the sleepy British countryside,
creating a great demand for
country hotels

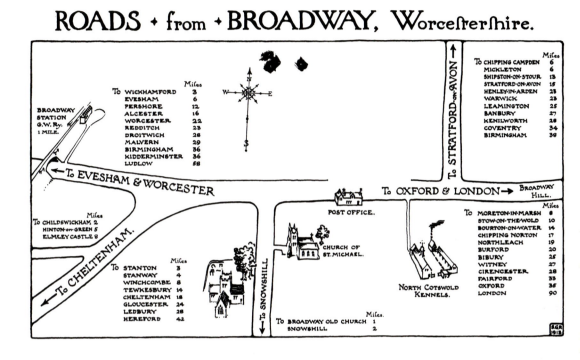

A map of the Broadway area drawn by Gordon Russell in 1913. Tucked into the Cotswold Hills, the village was surrounded by places with pleasant-sounding English names

ROADS ✦ from ✦ BROADWAY, Worcestershire.

BROADWAY STATION G.W. Ry. 1 MILE.

To	WICKHAMFORD	Miles
	WICKHAMFORD	3
	EVESHAM	6
	PERSHORE	12
	ALCESTER	16
	WORCESTER	22
	REDDITCH	23
	DROITWICH	26
	MALVERN	29
	BIRMINGHAM	36
	KIDDERMINSTER	36
	LUDLOW	58

← To EVESHAM & WORCESTER

	Miles
To CHILDSWICKHAM	2
HINTON-on-GREEN	5
ELMLEY CASTLE	8

To CHELTENHAM →

To	STANTON	Miles
	STANTON	3
	STANWAY	4
	WINCHCOMBE	8
	TEWKESBURY	14
	CHELTENHAM	18
	GLOUCESTER	24
	LEDBURY	26
	HEREFORD	42

To SNOWSHILL

POST OFFICE.

CHURCH OF ST. MICHAEL.

	Miles
To BROADWAY OLD CHURCH	1
SNOWSHILL	2

To OXFORD & LONDON →   BROADWAY HILL.

To STRATFORD-on-AVON

To	CHIPPING CAMPDEN	Miles
	CHIPPING CAMPDEN	6
	MICKLETON	6
	SHIPSTON-ON-STOUR	13
	STRATFORD-ON-AVON	15
	HENLEY-IN-ARDEN	23
	WARWICK	23
	LEAMINGTON	25
	BANBURY	27
	KENILWORTH	28
	COVENTRY	34
	BIRMINGHAM	39

NORTH COTSWOLD KENNELS.

To	MORETON-IN-MARSH	Miles
	MORETON-IN-MARSH	8
	STOW-ON-THE-WOLD	10
	BOURTON-ON-WATER	14
	CHIPPING NORTON	17
	NORTHLEACH	19
	BURFORD	20
	BIBURY	25
	WITNEY	27
	CIRENCESTER	28
	FAIRFORD	33
	OXFORD	35
	LONDON	90

to him that S B Russell named his youngest son Richard Drew Russell. Nobody involved in the deal could have had any idea of the impact that the investment would have on the future of British furniture design.

THE COTSWOLDS CAST THEIR SPELL

The move to Broadway marked one of the most influential turning-points in Gordon Russell's life. The excitement of the event is captured in this passage from *Designer's Trade*:

> For weeks beforehand we talked of nothing else. Twenty times a day we looked up Broadway on the map. We found out that there was a tower on top of Broadway Hill, that the nearest station was Evesham, that Stratford-on-Avon, Cheltenham and Worcester weren't far away, and that the villages nearby had pleasant English names – names which haunt one when far from England: Childswickham, Aston Subedge, Willersey, Hidcote Bartrim, Mickleton, Saintbury, Chipping Campden, Didbrook, Winchcombe. I was twelve, Don was ten, and Dick, my youngest brother, about six weeks old.

Gordon arrived in Broadway on 1 February 1904 with his two brothers, his mother and a Scottish nurse. They had travelled by train from Burton to Evesham via Birmingham and completed the last lap of their journey in a horse and trap. To a young boy with a vivid imagination, the Lygon Arms, with its atmosphere of antiquity and tradition, its carved stone fireplaces and rich plaster ceilings, must have been an enormous aesthetic and creative stimulant. The older parts of the inn date from the early sixteenth century. Oliver Cromwell is reputed to have slept there the night before the Battle of Worcester in 1651. The Hon John Byng wrote in *The Torrington Diaries* of a stay in the same room in 1787:

> There cannot be a cleanlier, civiller inn than this is; which bears all the marks of old gentility, and of having been a manor house; walls very thick, doors oaken and wide, with a profusion of timber, and the remains of much tapestry, for carpeting . . . My bedroom was very large with black oaken boards, a wrought ceiling, a wide cornice with a lofty mantle piece; in short I appear'd to be in the grand bedchamber of an old family seat.

S B Russell had read about the Lygon Arms in James John Hissey's *Across England in a Dog Cart*. He was attracted to this old house because he wanted to restore the inn's traditions, but his respect for history did not blind him to what lay ahead: he was one of the first businessmen at the turn of the century to recognize how the advent of the motor car would open up the sleepy British countryside and change the pattern of tourism. There would be great demand for country hotels such as the Lygon Arms. S B Russell's foresight and the uncompromising way in which he pushed forward with the restoration, using all the latest techniques, were characteristic of all Russell family dealings over the next 75 years. Whatever they did, they always moved forward and never looked back.

A pattern was swiftly established for young Gordon in Broadway. During the week he and Don were boarders at a grammar school in nearby Chipping Campden. At weekends he and his brother would walk the three or so miles back to Broadway and help out around the building yard and furniture repair shop that his father had established to restore the Lygon Arms to its former glory. Both school and home life influenced Gordon Russell profoundly in formulating his early interest in art, architecture and design. He found formal art classes at school to be uninspiring and aloof from the craft activity all around the area, but he took immense pleasure in Chipping Campden's architecture and sat up making sketches of buildings at night from his dormitory window. More than 70 years later he was to evoke the town scene of his schooldays with affection in an address entitled 'Skill', delivered to the Faculty of the Royal Designers for Industry at the Royal Society of Arts: 'It was a wonderful setting of splendid stone buildings forming a

Opposite: a doorway in the Lygon Arms. The hotel's atmosphere of antiquity and tradition inspired Gordon Russell's early interest in art and architecture. Above: the same doorway sketched by him

The Cromwell Room at
the Lygon Arms. Gordon
Russell's early sketchbook
captured the ornate
splendour of its fireplace

The inglenook at
the Lygon Arms,
reproduced by
Gordon Russell's
fine line. To a
young boy with a
vivid imagination
this new home was
a major creative
stimulant

One of the sketches made by Gordon Russell during his voyage to South America, which provided a magical interlude between school and working life in Broadway

street hard to match in Europe.' The Cotswolds had already started to exert on him the influence that would steer the course of his whole life. As he explains in *Designer's Trade*:

> I never cease to be grateful to my unknown but deeply revered teachers, the builders of these little Cotswold towns and villages. I came to them to learn and they taught me many things for lack of which the world is poorer today. They taught me that to build beautifully is quite different from beautifying a building. They taught me how to handle fine materials with respect. They taught me to employ direct, workmanlike methods and to try to apply the searching test of honesty to all work and actions.

Life at the Lygon Arms was equally inspiring. Gordon and Don were old enough to muck in, and Gordon in particular took an interest in the repair of antique furniture which so contributed to the Lygon's appeal. But Dick was still a baby and remained in the family's rented house at Snowshill while the rest of the Russells laboured long and hard to get the Lygon Arms into shape.

The way in which S B Russell, the former London bank clerk, threw himself vigorously into his new life at the age of 38 was little short of miraculous. He did not just make do and mend: he wanted the best and carried out everything with meticulous attention to visual quality no matter what the cost. Restoration work was carried out with great aesthetic care and sympathy for the inn's origins: coats of old wallpaper and matchboarding were stripped away, the Victorian windows replaced to match with original stone-mullioned ones, and unsightly pieces of furniture gradually replaced by a fine collection of old furniture, including many valuable antiques. S B Russell acquired Elizabethan oak tables, a Jacobean cupboard and some pieces of early Flemish tapestry to impress his guests. The impression made on young Gordon was certainly strong: he always credited his father with imbuing him with a love for old buildings and furniture, and an understanding of their construction and history.

A Working Life Begins

Gordon Russell's father had left school at 14 to work, so perhaps it was expected that the eldest son should join the family business as swiftly as possible. Gordon left school at the end of the Christmas term 1907 with no formal qualifications. He was 15. An uncle who was a sea captain arranged for Gordon to travel with him as a purser on a trip to South America aboard the *SS Veronese*. This first trip abroad, taking in the sights and sounds of Montevideo and Buenos Aires, must have been awe-inspiring, providing a magical interlude before getting down to the serious business of a working life in Broadway.

Back at the Lygon Arms the following April, Gordon Russell discovered there

A sketch of Broadway
rooftops made by Gordon
Russell from the Lygon Arms,
showing his fascination for
building and stonework

Gordon's mother, Elizabeth. Despite equalling her husband in dogged determination, she demanded a half bottle of champagne every evening to help her through the constant upheavals at the Lygon Arms

S B Russell, Gordon's father,
painted by Eric Kennington
in 1934. A stern, indomitable
figure, S B was known locally
as 'Rock' Russell for always
driving a hard bargain

was much to do. His father put him in charge of the skilled craftsmen in the repair workshop which serviced the interior of the hotel. This enterprise had been started by one craftsman, Jim Turner, and was to grow in size until it employed ten men by 1914. 'Everything had to be done differently,' Gordon wrote in *Designer's Trade*. 'By blood and sweat we found our own solutions as we went along. So interesting and infinitely varied was the work that it was not nearly as harassing as it sounds.'

S B Russell wanted his inn to be based on the country house model and to serve traditional, good quality English meals, rather than follow the 'bastard-French hotel tradition'. Whatever was needed to achieve their goal, the Russells would pursue it. They would search for good glassware, fabrics and cutlery, even commissioning pieces from craftsmen when they failed to track down what they wanted. They developed a thriving trade in antiques and, in 1907, even opened a small shop adjacent to the hotel to sell hand-picked and hand-restored items.

S B Russell's character was central to his son's early grounding in design appreciation. He was fierce with Gordon in his day-to-day demands but never less than encouraging in everything his son attempted to design or make. The hours were long but in the intoxicating atmosphere of the Lygon Arms, one senses a rich and infinitely varied life: one day spent in the workshop, the next out scouring the countryside for antiques. S B Russell was in some ways a cold and severe man. He began to suffer dreadfully from indigestion, which may have contributed to his grumpy disposition, and ate charcoal biscuits to ease the condition. He was known locally as 'Rock' Russell on account of his habit of concluding every market haggle over a sack of vegetables or two planks of wood with the phrase: 'Is that your rock-bottom price, is it?' A portrait in the Lygon Arms, painted in 1934 by Eric Kennington (see previous page), captures the man with stern demeanour and clenched fist. But he was also one of the most colourful and influential figures in the Broadway community. He ran the Post Office service for a time and was among the first telephone subscribers and motor car owners in the area. He had an innate grasp of how the modern age would creep up and change Broadway forever – and communicated that feeling of dynamic progress to his sons.

Gordon's mother took less interest in matters of art and architecture but she matched her husband for dogged single-mindedness. A frailer character might have been crushed between two such indomitable spirits, but Gordon rose to the challenge. An evidently serious boy who had no time for sports and enjoyed his own company, he cheerfully threw himself into work about the place and took full advantage of his freedom to absorb all that was going on in the area.

Within a few years of buying the Lygon Arms, Gordon Russell's father had commissioned the noted architect C E Bateman to design a new Great Hall for the inn (illustrated on page 24), to be used as a dining-room in summer and ballroom in winter. This was completed in 1909 and two years later a new bedroom wing to accommodate the growing number of people visiting Broadway

Jim Turner, the first furniture
craftsman employed by the
Russells. By 1914 the repair
workshop employed ten men

The Great Hall of the
Lygon Arms, designed by
C E Bateman and completed
in 1909. Gordon's father was
determined that the hotel
should be developed to the
highest aesthetic standards

by motor car was also built. Gordon Russell was fascinated by all the building trades involved in these extensions to the inn. 'Like most small boys,' he recalled in his 'Skill' lecture, 'I took pleasure from watching men and machines working. It was a way of discovering how ordinary people did ordinary jobs and made ordinary things.'

As a small boy, Gordon had liked to study and draw locomotives (see page 28). In the 'Skill' lecture he described one of the highlights of his youth as 'seeing one of Patrick Stirling's splendid Great North eight-foot singles steaming out of Burton-on-Trent Station in gleaming spring green, with all her brass shining.' Now he observed carpenters, blacksmiths, joiners, wagon-builders, stonemasons and silversmiths at close quarters. He wrote in his lecture: 'So much of it was the traditional work of the neighbourhood, done without fuss by men who, like Michelangelo, "sucked in chisels with their mother's milk".'

This vivid grounding in craft skills profoundly influenced Gordon Russell. He never lost his admiration for physical labour and manual skill. As he later recalled in the same lecture, he was particularly enamoured of a saying by Eric Gill: 'An artist is not a particular kind of person – each person is a particular kind of artist.' He intently studied the crafts all around him, read lots of books and swiftly became highly knowledgeable about all sorts of practical matters. Indeed, as a man of great physical strength and will, Gordon Russell often engaged in back-breaking work himself. He found value and fascination in the most mundane tasks – such as navvies breaking stones in the road – and discovered that firsthand observation of designer-makers at work at the bench was a more than adequate substitute for a formal design education. His close relationship with workshop craftsmen taught him the value of knowing how objects are produced so that his design drawings could correspond precisely with the making process. He was not allowed to forget the importance of this kind of communication: Jim Turner, the foreman, would hold his drawings up for light ridicule in the workshop if the sketch was not self-explanatory.

Gordon Russell was slowly emerging as one of the first modern designers of the twentieth century: he designed for others to make, using the fluent drawing skills he had developed since a small boy to communicate effectively with cabinet-makers and metalworkers. Amongst his earliest designs for the Lygon Arms were a simple oak bed in a recognizable Arts and Crafts style, made in about 1911, some silver buttons for the head porter and a handwritten statutory notice for guests. Gordon Russell was not, however, destined to become a master-maker himself. He lacked the physical subtlety and dexterity, as one set of poorly made bookcases from his youth demonstrated, but nevertheless tried his hand at all kinds

One of Gordon Russell's earliest designs for the Lygon Arms, circa 1911: an English oak bed in Arts and Crafts style

Gordon Russell and his father designed and produced this booklet to promote the Lygon's heritage. It was one of several small-scale publishing ventures whose guiding principle was typographic excellence

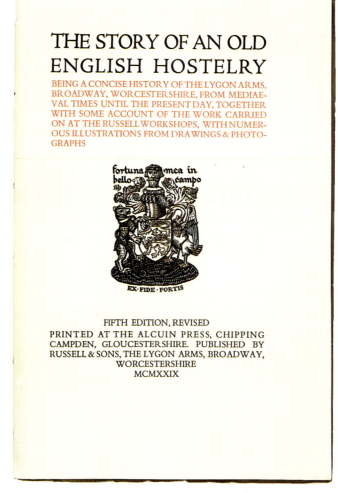

THE STORY OF AN OLD ENGLISH HOSTELRY

BEING A CONCISE HISTORY OF THE LYGON ARMS, BROADWAY, WORCESTERSHIRE, FROM MEDIAE-VAL TIMES UNTIL THE PRESENT DAY, TOGETHER WITH SOME ACCOUNT OF THE WORK CARRIED ON AT THE RUSSELL WORKSHOPS, WITH NUMER-OUS ILLUSTRATIONS FROM DRAWINGS & PHOTO-GRAPHS

fortuna mea in bello campo

EX·FIDE·FORTIS

FIFTH EDITION, REVISED
PRINTED AT THE ALCUIN PRESS, CHIPPING CAMPDEN, GLOUCESTERSHIRE. PUBLISHED BY RUSSELL & SONS, THE LYGON ARMS, BROADWAY, WORCESTERSHIRE
MCMXXIX

of crafts. Like his father, who was an expert amateur photographer and calligrapher, he experimented energetically with lettering and stonecarving. Together they designed and produced a high quality booklet to promote the unique heritage of the Lygon Arms to visitors. It was called *The Story of An Old English Hostelry* and was the first of the family's series of successful small-scale publishing ventures. Gordon also practised his calligraphic skills by creating a charming illuminated book of poems by Keats, which was given to a local bookbinder called Katherine Adams as a wedding present. She bound the book in the Eadburgha Bindery in Broadway and it survives to this day.

But these were only diversions. Essentially Gordon Russell prefigured the methods of a later generation of British product designers by developing – in a completely unselfconscious and rudimentary way – a shorthand between designer and maker based on fluent draughting skills. As his son-in-law Ken Baynes wrote in the book *Gordon Russell*, co-authored with Kate Baynes: 'His genius was to work in the way that brought out the best in the men who worked for him – challenging but never defying the inherent characteristics of the particular hand or machine skill he needed.' As a youth, Gordon Russell had always been a naturally talented artist. At the Lygon Arms he put that talent to practical use, guided by a father who possessed impeccable aesthetic judgement.

Just as Gordon was steered towards the running of the repair workshop and antiques business, so Don Russell was taken into the hotel to assist his father there. Both ventures benefited from the position of Broadway as base in the English countryside for a literary and artistic circle almost entirely made up of distinguished Americans. Such figures as Henry James, John Singer Sargent and Frank Millet had visited the village in the 1880s. Other well-known names were to follow, including the American actress Mary Anderson, J M Barrie, Ralph Vaughan Williams and Edward Elgar. S B Russell promoted his business to the American market by advertising the Lygon Arms on the Cunard liners. By 1914 large numbers of antiques, including ornamental gates, were leaving Broadway station destined for shipment to America. Henry Ford was one of the earliest customers. He stayed a number of times at the Lygon, and after World War One the Russells sold him several items for his Detroit museum, including parts of a Cotswolds blacksmith's shop.

Towel rails designed for the Lygon Arms in 1911. The different finishes and detailing show how Gordon Russell's craft was developing during this period

ARTS, CRAFTS AND INDUSTRY

Gordon Russell was fortunate in coming to the Cotswolds at exactly the time that it was emerging as a centre for resurgent Arts and Crafts activity. Many of the Arts and Crafts Movement's leading figures had chosen to settle in the area on account of its natural beauty, and Gordon unwittingly found himself caught at the centre of the debate about the role of handwork in design. The Arts and Crafts Movement had developed in England as a protest against mid-Victorian industrialization, which had displaced the small-town craftsman as provider of local domestic objects and furniture. According to William Morris, the principal spokesman of the Arts and Crafts Movement, manufacturing had de-skilled the labour force with disastrous social and aesthetic consequences, and industry had ruined craft.

Morris lived in a manor house at Kelmscott, a mere 30 miles from Broadway, and one of his most faithful disciplines, Ernest Gimson, lived nearer still – at Sapperton, just 20 miles away. Gimson, a trained architect, had moved to the area with London furniture-makers Ernest and Sidney Barnsley one year before the Russells bought the Lygon Arms. The work of Gimson and the Barnsleys stands among the finest of the Arts and Crafts period: honest, well-made furniture with, in the case of Gimson, a good deal of originality and sophistication.

Unlike his father, Gordon Russell never met Ernest Gimson but both came into contact with another Arts and Crafts group, the Campden Guild, established in 1902 and led by C R Ashbee, also a fervent follower of Morris. When Gordon Russell joined a small life-drawing class in Campden, he came into contact with a number of the Guild's members, including the sculptor Alec Miller, the brothers Will (a woodcarver) and George Hart (a silversmith), and the artist and engraver Fred Griggs.

Clearly the Arts and Crafts Movement made a stylistic impression on Gordon Russell's work, but its ideology was to be only a starting-point for the principles which shaped his life and work. Within a few years he had totally and irrevocably departed from its anti-industrial stance. Although he warned in his 'Skill' lecture, 'We deprive a man of his skill at our peril', he was wary of the central tenets of the Arts and Crafts philosophy:

> I saw that the Arts and Crafts leaders were trying to bring designer and maker together, in itself a most worthy objective, but by insisting that the craftsman should design everything that he made they went a bit too far . . . it became clear that the designer must have a thorough knowledge of methods of production, whether by hand or machine.

He was also suspicious of the Movement's distaste for businessmen and the fact

As a small boy Gordon Russell liked to study and draw locomotives: knowing how things worked was of the utmost importance to him

6- coupled Tank Engine . F.C.CA, S. America
Built in 1907, by Beyer, Peacock & Co, Manchester
Guage 5' 6'.

that the rural isolation which its followers enjoyed was all
the easier for the private incomes earned by their families
in industry. In the years before war shattered the peace
of rural England, Gordon Russell was gradually evolving
a personal outlook destined to shape the direction of
his future furniture company. Like his father, he was
obsessively interested in quality and appreciated the
spiritual value of work, yet he failed to see why things
which could be swiftly and easily done by machine should
be done by hand, or why furniture and objects should be
so painstaking and expensive to produce that only the
wealthy could afford them. Although his aims were not yet
as clearly formulated as they became in the 1920s, when
he declared his intention 'to make decent furniture for
ordinary people', the formative influences of his early years
had already made their mark by the time war was declared
in August 1914.

THE HORRORS OF WAR

When the news of war finally broke, Gordon was
characteristically absorbed in a craft activity, writing
a copy of *Omar Khayyam* on vellum in a small workroom
he had set up. However, recalling his earlier South American voyage which had
given him a 'taste for travel' and believing war to be romantic, he signed up with
a territorial battalion of the Worcesters within a month.

Soldier sons:
Gordon (right)
and Don Russell in
uniform. Both were
wounded in action
but both survived

The war started slowly: Gordon spent a 'fine autumn' billeted in Worcester.
But the following March his battalion was sent to the front line in France. 'I felt
that we had cut ourselves off from normal life and entered a mad world,' he wrote
in *Designer's Trade*. The experiences of World War One had such a profound and
devastating effect on Gordon Russell that when he came to begin his memoirs in
the 1940s, he was unsure whether to chronicle the full horrors or to omit his years
in the trenches altogether. He eventually decided to include a chapter on his war
experiences and this gives us an insight into what it must have been like to endure
a living hell for years on end, living in a sea of mud with the stench of death and
scenes of carnage and destruction all around.

Gordon Russell miraculously survived the battles of Loos, Passchendaele,
Somme and Ypres. He rose through the ranks to become a commissioned officer
in 1917, describing himself in his army officer's record book as a 'Designer of
Furniture'. This was, he remarked in *Designer's Trade*, 'an expression of hope rather
than a statement of fact !' He was later shot in the left arm, awarded the Military
Cross, 'which didn't come up with the rations', and ended the war with the
commendation of his commanding officer etched in his record book: 'Lt Russell is

A war drawing by Gordon Russell, showing that even amid the horrors of the trenches he never lost his sense of humour, nor his powers of observation

a capable and fearless officer, with great influence among men.' Indeed one of the skills which Gordon Russell evidently honed amid the mind-numbing brutality of war was the ability to motivate and organize the rank and file. In his obituary of Gordon Russell in the *Architectural Review,* John Gloag, an editor who gave Gordon valuable advice in the 1920s, commented on how the war 'enlarged his knowledge of men and their moods, their strengths and weaknesses'.

The landscape of war left Gordon Russell mentally scarred: although he would continue to enjoy country walks, he would never again stride off down muddy paths as he had in his youth, for they were a painful reminder of experiences in the trenches. But, remarkably, even in the trenches, he had studied plans for a house his father had bought at nearby Snowshill and written detailed reports on the renovation work to be carried out. He had also observed the concrete gun emplacements and pillboxes of the Germans, and in the midst of all the horror and destruction, made a mental note of their texture – a design which he would use more than 50 years later in his own garden. This says much about the character of the man: he remained absorbed in how things were made, their form and their natural beauty, and even while enduring the most terrible conditions imaginable; with death all around, he never lost the sense of himself as a young man living in the Cotswolds, every day watching dry-stone wallers, stonemasons and weavers at work.

When the war ended, every town and village in England counted its war dead. The losses were huge – yet Gordon had survived even the bloodiest campaigns, as had his brother Don, who was also wounded. Their mother, when asked if it wasn't a miracle that both her soldier sons had emerged unscathed, retorted sharply: 'Of course I knew they would !' It was a typically assured response. Douglas Barrington, an Australian serviceman who was later befriended by Don Russell during World War Two and knew the Russell family well, comments: 'For Mrs Russell there were two sorts of people in the world – the Russells and the others.'

Gordon Russell returned to Broadway saddened that 'more than a million of my generation, among them most of my schoolfriends and men I had lived with, would remain in the fields of France'. In *Designer's Trade* he described his strong feeling at the time that 'my generation, which had destroyed so much lovely work, had a constructive duty to perform; somehow or other we had to hand on to those coming after us good things of our own creation'. While serving in the army he had concentrated his thoughts on furniture design. In the years which followed he would translate those thoughts into deeds.

Chapter 2

TEACHING *the* MACHINE MANNERS

This page and opposite: the English walnut cabinet which won a gold medal at the 1925 Paris International Exhibition. Designed by Gordon Russell in Arts and Crafts style, it is inlaid with ebony, yew and box

Gordon Russell's father greeted the return of his sons from World War One by changing the name of the family firm from S B Russell to Russell & Sons. Don's pre-war commitment to the Lygon Arms was rewarded with a role in managing the hotel's affairs; Gordon was formally assigned to revive the antique business and run the workshop, although Don was also free to buy antiques for the Lygon and became highly expert at it. The arrangement gave Gordon exactly the opportunity he needed to put into practice ideas he had developed while in the Worcestershire Regiment, above all his ambition to produce his own designs. He explains his reasons in *Designer's Trade*:

> To me it was a poor age that could make no contribution of its own. I argued that if the eighteenth century had been content to imitate the seventeenth, then the finest age of English cabinet making would never have been born . . . I had far too much respect for the past not to be revolted by the regurgitations I saw on all sides. I had no qualifications beyond a burning belief that my own age might recover its self-respect, a sound knowledge of old furniture and construction and an interest in the possibilities of the machine.

The workshop at Broadway, which, after seeking expert advice, Gordon Russell reorganized for his own furniture manufacturing

MAKING A NAME IN FURNITURE

When Dick, the youngest Russell, left school, he joined Gordon's side of the family business. Dick was to prove an important ally in his elder brother's efforts to develop modern furniture designs. When the Russells bought an old farmhouse about a hundred yards down the road from the Lygon Arms to convert into showrooms for their antiques, one begins to sense two competing businesses within one family, mutually dependent but always fighting their own corner. Which one did S B Russell favour most? Douglas Barrington, an intimate of the family for many years and the Lygon's eventual owner, comments:

> Mr S B Russell favoured Gordon and sometimes cooked the books so that the workshops made a profit and the hotel showed a loss when it was really the other way around. Don respected Gordon but he was also infuriated by him. Gordon always seemed to be the one spending the money.

Both Gordon and Don had returned from service in the field with a heightened awareness of the common man. They campaigned, for instance, to reopen the public bar at the Lygon Arms for the locals at the very time their father was targeting the inn at well-heeled, refined visitors. In Gordon's case, the concern for Everyman translated itself into the desire to produce furniture not just for the wealthy but for everyone to afford. Inevitably that would eventually mean making use of the machine and going against the tenets of the Arts and Crafts Movement, which so flavoured his boyhood.

The problem was that Broadway had no history of cabinet-making. The men in the workshop were essentially joiners repairing seventeenth-century furniture. This problem taxed Gordon Russell considerably, but he was determined to find a way forward. He joined the Design and Industries Association, which introduced him to a wide range of new people and influences. Then, in the early 1920s, he designed some original pieces of bedroom furniture, which showed a stylistic debt

Bedroom furniture designed
by Gordon Russell in the
early 1920s, showing a
stylistic debt to Ashbee
and Gimson

to Ashbee and Gimson. He had the furniture produced in the workshops and photographed by his father. Armed with the photographs he travelled to London to seek the advice of two men who were to prove instrumental in shaping his future career.

The first was John Gloag, an architectural historian who was then assistant editor of the trade newspaper *The Cabinet Maker*. Gloag had come to Gordon's attention via the Design and Industries Association. He was encouraging and agreed to feature the work in an article. Years later he described Gordon Russell's work of the period in evocative terms:

> It was as recognizably English as roast beef, Stilton cheese and the beer that used to be served in English pubs. Untainted by old-world sentimentality, such furniture gained in mellowness from the passage of time, for wood untreated by stains and indifferent French polishing acquires depth and richness of colour. (*Architects' Journal*, 15 August 1928)

Gordon Russell's second adviser was Percy Wells, head of cabinet-making at the LCC Shoreditch Technical Institute. The two had met prior to 1914 when Wells, a distant relative of Mrs S B Russell, was visiting the Cotswolds. Percy Wells had a wealth of practical advice to impart. On his recommendation, Gordon Russell sent one of his own staff, Jim Turner's son Edgar, to Shoreditch to train as a cabinet-maker rather than bring in an outsider. The decision was also taken to separate the workshop involved in making new pieces from the original repair shop.

Wells not only gave valuable advice, but also sent a number of Shoreditch-trained cabinet-makers to help out at Broadway. Among them was a 17-year-old lad called W H 'Curly' Russell (no relation to Gordon). 'Curly' was destined to take over the running of the drawing office in the late 1920s before going on to become chief designer for the Gordon Russell company for many years until his retirement in 1968.

Supported by John Gloag and Percy Wells, Gordon Russell began to move outside the closed world of the Cotswolds and in the early 1920s he gradually

Workers' cottages built by the Russells in 1927 to house their growing workforce. Ten of the twelve cottages were destroyed by fire seven years later

started making his entrance on the larger stage of British design. An exhibition of his work at a Cheltenham Arts and Crafts show in 1922 resulted the following year in an invitation from the Department of Overseas Trade to design a model café in the North Court of the Victoria and Albert Museum in London. Gordon Russell's café ('a bit rustic and unfinished' in his view) appeared alongside a room furnished by Heal's. A friendship developed between the firms and Ambrose Heal's son Anthony subsequently spent time working at Broadway.

After the V&A exhibition, the pace of change quickened for Gordon Russell. His name now began

One of the awards that Gordon Russell brought back from the 1925 Paris Exhibition during his swift development from Cotswolds obscurity to international acclaim

to acquire the status of a quality cabinet-maker. He designed an entire dining-room for his first private patron (Albert Hartley of Rochdale), and in 1924 he was invited to exhibit at the British Empire Exhibition at Wembley. Centrepiece of this display was a walnut cabinet on an ebony base made by Edgar Turner while he was training at Shoreditch. That year the workshop expanded to 30 employees.

In 1925 Russell & Sons showed at the British pavilion of the Paris Exhibition and won three medals (one gold and two silver) for its work. The gold award winner, a walnut cabinet, was strongly reminiscent of Ernest Gimson. Gimson had proved to Gordon Russell that it was possible to make good, honest furniture which avoided imitating furniture of the past (just as Ambrose Heal had shown him that there was a commercial market for it). It was Russell's love and respect for the quality of old furniture that inspired him to design original new pieces.

Despite the ever-present Arts and Crafts influence, Gordon Russell's design philosophy was becoming increasingly modern. He supported his new direction with a pamphlet, which he wrote and illustrated himself in 1923. It was called *Honesty and The Crafts – A Plea for a Broader Outlook* and set out his manifesto for modern design in envigorating style:

> Is there indeed so great a gulf fixed between the faking of houses and furniture and the faking of £5 notes? Are we to admire things because they are beautiful, or because they are old? The doctrine that nothing is beautiful unless it is old has created an army of swindlers, whose artful work may in time even bring discredit on the lovely craftsmanship which they attempt to imitate. It is therefore high time that we paid some attention to the question of reproductions which seem to be the present fashionable craze.

It must be remembered that there was shrill opposition to modern design and architecture in the England of the early 1920s. 'Practically every retailer – except

Heal's and Dunn's of Bromley – laughed at the idea and prophesied an early cessation of such nonsense,' recalled Gordon Russell in his 'Skill' lecture at the RSA. However, the rural splendour of the Lygon Arms was attracting a more discerning, well-to-do customer to Broadway. These people perhaps understood more readily what the Russells were trying to achieve and had the money to support it. At that time, Gordon knew instinctively that educating the buying public, the retail trade and other manufacturers in his way of thinking was important. Later in his career, he would devote his life entirely to that end as Director of the Council of Industrial Design.

A CONVINCING DESIGNER

The 1920s marked the zenith of Gordon Russell's career as a designer. He designed not only furniture but also beautiful glassware and metalwork, all of which went on sale in the Lygon Cottage showrooms near the Lygon Arms. His output was prolific. In May 1927 an exhibition of his work at James Powell & Sons in Wigmore Street, London prompted *The Studio* magazine to write: 'His designs are always virile and convincing. While definitely individual in character and modern in conception they exhibit the fundamental sanity and restraint which are characteristic of our native craftsmanship in the past. He never resorts to tricks.'

A vivid portrait of Russell around this time comes from Val Freeman, who joined the company in 1925 as a showroom cashier at Broadway and subsequently spent 44 years working there in a succession of senior sales jobs. Freeman had answered an advertisement in the Situations Vacant column of the *Birmingham Post* and recalls being taken in to see Gordon Russell on his first day at work:

Mirror stand with three drawers and ratchet adjustment mechanism dating from the 1920s, Gordon Russell's most prolific period as a designer

> Mr Gordon had a drawing-board on his knee and a pencil in his hand. He was clad in a blue herring-bone jacket, matching knickerbockers gartered at the knee, a blue shirt and red tie. His stockings were a shade of mauve and his shoes were brown brogues. He wore round rimless spectacles with steel earpieces. His hair was quite dark, cut short and parted across the forehead. He said simply: 'I hope you'll be happy and we'll do everything we can to make it so'.

There were 36 people in the company at that time. Freeman recalls how Gordon was greatly admired by his employees and took great interest in them and their families. 'He always knew if there was a baby on the way or anything like that.' Yet Gordon was still very much under the influence of his father and hated going against his wishes. He was also wrestling with the traditional design legacy of his upbringing in the Cotswolds, but in this he was soon to achieve a breakthrough.

The 1925 Paris gold award winner may have reflected the deep-rooted craft techniques and traditions of the Broadway furniture workshops, but a flush-fronted boot cupboard of the same year marked a radical departure in style. Made

Above: the
Lygon Cottage
showrooms at
Broadway in
the late 1920s.
Left: chest of
drawers designed
by Gordon Russell
for Lloyd George
and made from a
holly tree growing
in the politician's
own garden

Gordon Russell's
range as a designer
extended to
glassware and
metalware. Above:
Stanway pale blue
table glass, 1927.
Below: metal dish,
designed in 1924

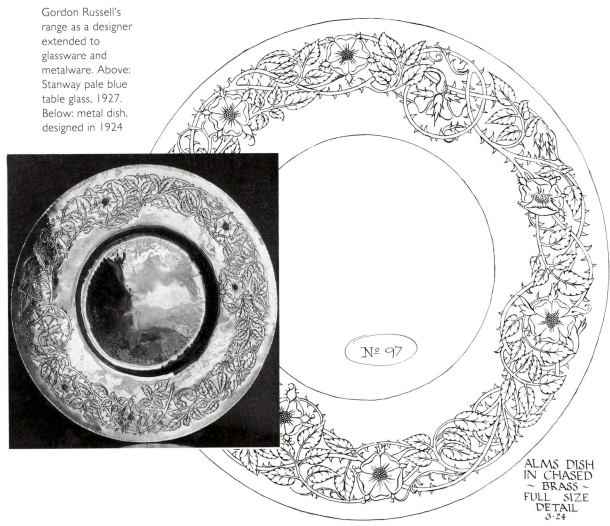

№ 97

ALMS DISH
IN CHASED
~ BRASS ~
FULL SIZE
DETAIL
3·24

Oakleaf wall sconce, 1926.
The same year Russell joined
the Art Workers' Guild,
where he exchanged ideas
with many other craftsmen

Decorative cup
and cover in heavy
polished bronze,
1923. Russell's
design drawings
were simple for
skilled craftsmen
to follow

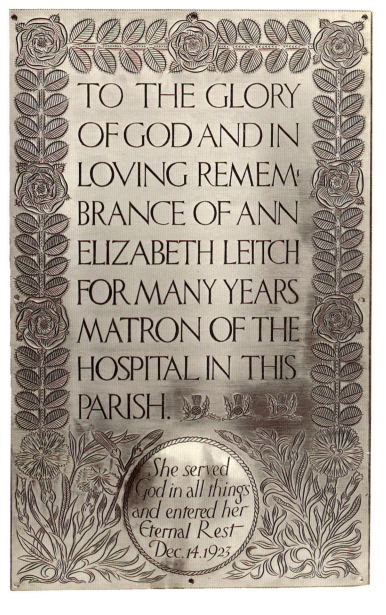

Commemorative plaque, candelabra and butcher's sign – examples of Gordon Russell's metalwork designs, which became a conspicuous local feature during the 1920s

from Cuban mahogany with veneered blockboard doors, its geometric simplicity prefigured future utilitarian and functional approaches to form and finish, not only in Russell furniture but in British design as a whole. When the design historian Gillian Naylor wrote a history of the company, she described the boot cupboard as being remarkable for its anticipation of 'a vocabulary that was to be used by British furniture designers throughout the 1950s . . . From the 1920s the history of Russell furniture becomes part of the history of British design in the twentieth century.'

Architectural historian Nikolaus Pevsner has added to the mystery of the futuristic boot cupboard. In *Studies in Art, Architecture and Design* he reveals Russell's explanation that the cupboard was 'guided by certain eighteenth-century precedents – wardrobes with flush veneered doors built of reversed mahogany strips – and by occasional flush Gimson pieces, such as a chest of about 1916.'

History clearly informed Gordon Russell's work, but here was a genuinely original talent reaching out to an ever-wider audience. In 1926 came a contract to refurbish the library at King's College, Aberdeen, the first of many large-scale jobs in the education market. In the same year, Russell joined the Art Workers' Guild, partly at the suggestion of Percy Wells. Founded in 1884 by the great architect and designer C F A Voysey, the Guild provided a meeting-place for artists, architects and craftsmen. It was a lively forum which influenced Russell's outlook, although by then Gordon Russell was, in his own words, 'shot at from both sides': the Arts and Crafts Society scorned the introduction of machines into the workshops, while the mainstream trade pilloried the modern design he championed. But Gordon Russell appeared to relish the role of pioneer. His move into batch production, treating the machine as 'just a more complex tool', made him still more frustrated with the anti-industrial philosophy of William Morris, just as the gradual replacement of antiques with contemporary designs in his business led to a radical reassessment of the role of the craftsman.

Pevsner describes how machines for series production – a planer, followed by a circular saw, a band saw, an Elliot woodworker and a dimension bench saw – were introduced to Broadway in the mid-1920s. But the atmosphere was still that of a workshop, not a factory, and run according to Russell's belief that 'the most urgent job of all was to teach the machine manners'. Experiences in the army had taught him the value of good communications, so he organized a series of lectures on various subjects for workshop staff. Guest speakers included silversmith George Hart, cabinet-maker Percy Wells and C F A Voysey, then in his seventies.

Above: the
expanding cabinet-
making shop in
1927, showing
the first signs of
mechanization.
Left: Russell's
mysterious boot
cupboard of 1925,
prefiguring many
of the geometric
concerns of 1950s
British design

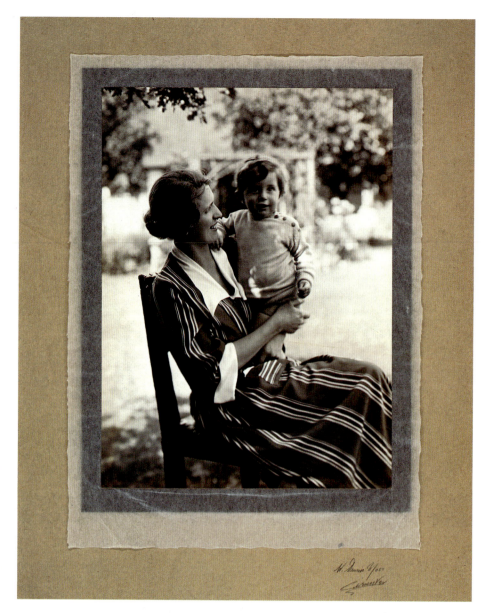

Top: Toni, Gordon Russell's wife, with one of her three sons. Life at Broadway and later at Kingcombe demanded physical and mental stamina in equal measure. Bottom: marriage bed, designed by Gordon and made by Edgar Turner

In the *Architects' Journal* of January 1926 Wells wrote encouragingly of Gordon Russell's use of machinery: 'He is not blind to its abuses, but he recognizes its right place in saving hard and back-breaking labour. He uses machinery but controls it, and his furniture is such as will leave the craftsman scope for individual interest, intelligence and skill, either in the simplest or the most elaborate examples.' Wells believed that however good a design might look on paper, its ultimate success depended on cooperation and communication with the maker. He commented on Gordon Russell: 'His men work not so much for him as with him.'

MARRIAGE AND KINGCOMBE

If the changes in the company were dramatic in the 1920s, then the changes in the man were no less so. Gordon Russell changed from a shy, rather solitary and unfocused young man with a sympathy for old things and an interest in practical ones into one of the most forward-thinking and best-known figures in modern British design. His confidence and creative powers grew visibly during the decade as his enterprise, backed by the income of the Lygon Arms, took shape. One of the key factors in this transformation must have been his marriage in August 1921 to Toni Denning, an Irish doctor's daughter who a year before had answered an advertisement for a secretarial job at Broadway and joined the company. 'She seemed very interested in the advertisement because it seemed an unusual job,' wrote Gordon in *Designer's Trade*. 'Poor wretch! She little dreamed of the depths of unusualness to which the job might sink.'

Toni Denning had grown up in a family of Plymouth Brethren and, according to her daughter Kate, had experienced a harsh, practical Victorian childhood not dissimilar to Gordon's own. Certainly she appeared well-equipped to cope with conditions in Broadway, which demanded stamina and intelligence in equal measure. When Gordon came to revise his autobiography a year or two before he died, retitling it *Designer's Education*, he paid tribute to the way Toni encouraged his early work as a furniture designer: 'Her steadfast belief that my ideas could be accomplished was a great source of support to me in their development.' He also recalled an amusing incident in which he and his brother Don, on hearing that an attractive young woman had been invited by their father for interview and put up overnight in S B Russell's Snowshill home, paid a deliberate early morning visit to catch a glimpse of her:

> We found a very good-looking girl with a head of long, golden hair, quite unabashed by this mainly masculine group. In fact she later told me that she had found it extremely difficult not to burst out laughing when she saw two large men appear, sit on joint stools and eat their porridge and cream out of little silver bowls.

Gordon and Toni were married at St Martin-in-the-Fields Church, London. Gordon even designed the marriage bed, which was made in the workshop by

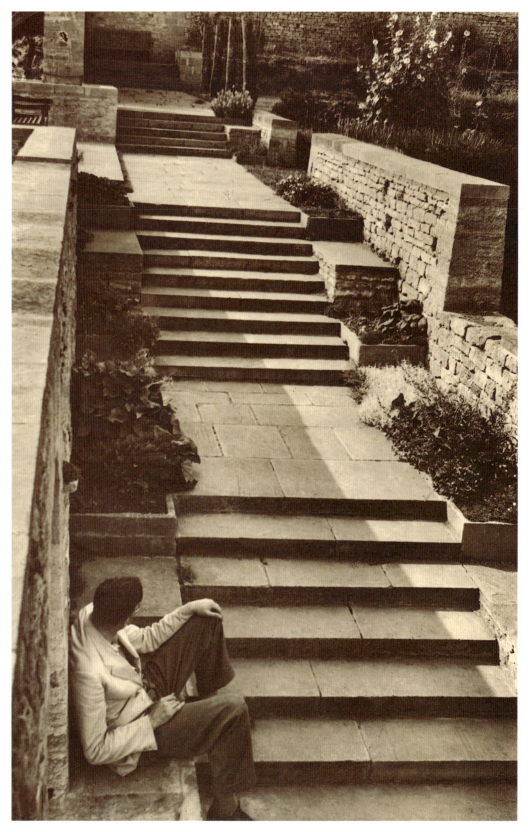

Gordon Russell
surveys his
handiwork at
Kingcombe,
where he indulged
his passion for
landscape
gardening

Edgar Turner. Val Freeman remembers the impact that Toni Russell had around the place in the 1920s : 'She was a perfect charmer, cheerful, lively and nice-looking with bright blue eyes which she was very good at using. She was always very involved with her husband.'

Gordon and Toni Russell began their married life in a cottage adjoining the Lygon Arms, but by 1924 they already had two small boys, Michael and Robert, and the need for their own home was pressing. Two more children, Oliver and a daughter, Kate, were to follow. Gordon Russell wanted to build his own house in the hills near Broadway and so he and his wife began to look out for suitable sites. In the summer of 1924 Toni Russell went to inspect a site at the crossroads near Dover's Hill above Chipping Campden. Gordon Russell's own pencil-written notes of the period describe their attraction to the place: 'I remembered the field as I had walked up Dyer's Lane many scores of times since my first visit to Campden in 1904. I liked it as much as she did and we found there was what appeared to be a small spring in one corner on Kingcombe Lane.'

The Russells commissioned architect Leslie Mansfield to design the house in local stone on the 'isolated site with which we had already fallen in love' – and where there was no mains sewerage or electricity. Gordon cut the first sod on Boxing Day 1924 and building work began early in 1925. The Russells moved into Kingcombe in May 1926. In his notes, Gordon professed himself 'delighted with really sunny house and singing of the birds'. It was to be the family home for the next half century.

As there was no garden, Gordon – a man of towering physique – started levelling terraces close to the house by hand. The laborious job was to take up his spare time for several years. Encouraged by his parents, he became passionately interested in plants and garden landscaping, and 'began to see house, garden and landscape as a whole.' He read widely on the subject and, by the late 1920s, one senses that his creative energies were gradually being diverted from the furniture company towards his unusual home and steeply inclined garden. The picture of Gordon Russell working on his garden at Kingcombe is one which many who knew him well still carry with them. It adds another facet to an already multi-faceted character and reveals a man of immense physicality as well as a man of ideas. In the introduction to their book, *Gordon Russell*, his son-in-law Ken Baynes and daughter Kate wrote: 'To have seen him at home, up to his knees in mud excavating his garden canal next to an Irish casual labourer and an expert joiner, was to experience something almost feudal in character.'

Life at Kingcombe, with its endless jobs to be carried out, became a haven for Gordon Russell away from ever greater commercial pressures at work. Kingcombe increasingly assumed the focus for his design skills and architectural interests as

Kingcombe, the family home, designed by Leslie Mansfield: this private environment became a focal point for Gordon Russell's creative energy for the next 50 years

the designing of furniture at Broadway, which he had largely monopolized since 1919, started to become the province of others, most notably his brother Dick. In later life Kingcombe would be the centre of creative renaissance for a man who stopped designing furniture in 1930 and, remarkably, did not resume for 47 years.

MAKING WAY FOR MODERNITY

Gordon Russell's abrupt decision to stop designing at the end of the 1920s was due in part to the growing complexity of the Broadway operation. Despite the progress made during his first few years in business, he was not satisfied with the persisting reliance on craft techniques, nor with the heavy workload of both designing and managing which fell on his albeit broad shoulders. He was aware of the potential benefit to be gained from an architectural influence, summing up in *Designer's Trade*: 'Looking back at the men who had done interesting furniture under the inspiration of William Morris' teaching – men such as Lethaby, Voysey, Mackintosh, Ashbee, Heal, Gimson and Sidney and Ernest Barnsley – I noticed that all but Heal were architects. This could hardly be a coincidence.'

Typically, the solution to the problem was found within the Russell family. In 1927 Gordon persuaded his father to send Dick to the Architectural Association in London to study as an architect for four years. The two brothers had discussed such a move during the long country walks they frequently enjoyed together. Dick's architectural training was a stroke of genius on Gordon Russell's part and was to have a major effect on the future of his furniture company. His brother's natural talent blossomed in London, marking the start of a process which led him later to become an eminent consultant designer for industry, a Royal College of Art professor in wood, metal and plastics, and one of the most important, if underrated, figures in twentieth-century British design.

Almost immediately, Dick Russell brought valuable skills and contacts back to Broadway from the Architectural Association. Notable young designers such as Eden Minns, David Booth, Jimmie Wilson, Robert Goodden, Sandro Girard and Marian Pepler began to exert an influence on the company in the late 1920s. Marian Pepler, as Dick's future wife, became most intimately connected with the Russell family. She was the daughter of Sir George Pepler, an architect, town planner and founder member of the Town Planning Institute. Like Dick, her training at the AA was to a large extent dictated: her father wanted her to study the architecture of housing so she could become an architectural modelmaker. Instead she became one of Europe's finest designers of modern carpets and rugs, and in the 1930s her work often complemented Gordon Russell furniture.

According to Marian Pepler, Dick talked little of the family business while at the AA, even though his background in practical furniture-making and architectural restoration at the Lygon Arms surely provided a useful counterpoint to the architectural theory which dominated their studies. At some point, however, he must have made public his desire to bring back to Broadway something of the new design culture of the AA, as there was soon a steady stream of eager, bright-eyed AA graduates knocking on Gordon Russell's door. They were passionate about new ideas in modern design and would talk endlessly about such topics as the Bauhaus, Le Corbusier and Frank Lloyd Wright, while holidaying at the Snowshill home of Dick's parents. Marian found Gordon rather precious and offputting on first meeting but later they formed a close personal and professional relationship. 'Gordon was very far-sighted in the people he involved in the company at that time,' she recalls.'He was always willing to give a designer with new ideas a chance. That included Dick.'

It gradually became clear that Russell & Sons, renamed the The Russell Workshops in November 1927, was widening its horizons beyond the insular Cotswolds craft community. Through the medium of Dick Russell's architectural training at the AA, it had become exposed to exciting new ideas which were linked to the Modern Movement and international in scope. Yet, as Ken and Kate Baynes comment in their book on Gordon Russell:

> The theories of the Modern Movement were never swallowed whole at Broadway. Throughout the intensive period of innovation and experiment that was about to begin, a strong sense of tradition and an insistence on the highest possible standards of craftsmanship maintained a bedrock of common sense.

By now a new company had been formed to separate the furniture-making side of the family business from the affairs of the Lygon Arms, and an efficient company secretary, R H Bee, was appointed to handle accountancy and administration. In September 1929 the company name was changed again: from the The Russell Workshops to Gordon Russell Ltd. This, Gordon Russell explained in *Designer's Trade,* was 'because the former title was felt to have a somewhat exclusive, handmade air whereas the latter tied up with the writing and lecturing I was doing as well as the fact that we had started to develop well-made and well-designed things – things of quality – which were produced by machine to a considerable extent.'

1929 was also the year that Marian Pepler graduated from the AA and Dick Russell – by then running the drawing office at Gordon Russell Ltd – received his first architectural commission. This was for a house at Follifoot near Harrogate in Yorkshire. The client was Albert Hartley, who had six years earlier provided Gordon Russell with his first order for an entire coordinated dining-room. Hartley's patronage of the Russells can be seen as a bridge between the old cabinet-making tradition and the new architectural approach to interior design prevalent

When The Russell Workshops were renamed Gordon Russell Ltd in 1929, the logo, with its rural craft associations (shown on the van below) was replaced by the more mechanistic Circular Saw

Lobden, a private house in the Malvern Hills, designed in the International Style by Dick Russell and Marian Pepler, 1932

within the company by the end of the 1920s. Follifoot was a fairly conventional forerunner to a second house for Albert Hartley, Lobden in the Malvern Hills, designed by Dick Russell and Marian Pepler in 1932. With its flat roof, modern geometric furnishings (with furniture by Gordon Russell) and white exterior walls (albeit made of brick, not Modernist concrete), Lobden reflected the progressive new movements sweeping European architecture and design. Recalling the house's development for the Dick Russell and Marian Pepler exhibition at the Geffrye Museum in London 50 years later, Marian observed that Lobden had been influenced by illustrations of Le Corbusier's Villa Savoye and Gropius' house at Dessau. Gordon Russell's enterprise was now in the vanguard of European Modernism. Just ten years previously it had been part of the local Arts and Crafts scene in the Cotswolds. The transformation was truly remarkable.

Such rapid change may partly explain why at the end of the 1920s Gordon Russell took a back seat in designing for his own furniture company. The likeliest theory is that he felt ill-equipped to design in the same simple, modern idiom as Dick Russell and the other AA-trained architects. Dick Russell had been made a director of the company in August 1928 and a feature of Gordon's career noted by many was that he could always appreciate good work by others without interfering in its execution. But there is also the possibility that he was eased out, caught in a pincer movement between the AA graduates' skills in designing for machine production and the tighter financial and technical control instituted by R H Bee, the company secretary.

There is, however, no trace of self-pity in Gordon Russell's writings of the period, just as there is none in any of his other written work. He simply set his sights on the next challenge to be faced and forged boldly ahead with other company projects. There was, of course, a great deal to think about. Twelve workers' cottages, designed by Leslie Mansfield, were erected in 1927 to house a growing workforce. Meanwhile a contract market of sorts was beginning to emerge as schools, universities and hospitals bought Russell furniture ranges. Professor Attenborough of Leicester University – father of David and Richard – was among the early customers. Then there were the prestigious visitors who included Henry Ford and the future Queen Mother, whose aunt Lady Maud Bowes-Lyon lived in Broadway. It was hardly a dull time.

The business had moved a long way from purely servicing the Lygon, but it

Left: the living room at Lobden, with interrior furnishings supplied by Gordon Russell Ltd, illustrating the progressive design ideas sweeping Europe. Below: sitting room of one of the company's workers' cottages

Top: Gordon
Russell Ltd's
first London
showroom, opened
in October 1929
at 28 Wigmore
Street. Bottom:
brochure from the
late 1920s showing
designs for English
walnut bedroom
furniture

still experienced sticky financial patches, and would continue to do so in the 1930s. Faced with a large bank overdraft during one of the more serious phases, Gordon Russell capitalized on his ability to mobilize support for his beliefs within the business community: he was given an on-the-spot £12,000 loan by Cecil Pilkington with no strings attached. By today's standards, the sum would be more like £350,000. 'Pay it back when you are over the hump,' Cecil Pilkington told him. 'Worthwhile concerns are built up by your kind of drive.'

Gordon Russell was a driven man and expansion always appeared uppermost in his mind. In 1928, when staging another London one-man show at the Arlington Gallery in Bond Street, it dawned on him that the retail showrooms at Broadway were rather limiting his horizons. By now the company employed 120 people, and traded in glass and textiles as well as furniture. On 1 October 1929 the company opened a London showroom at 28 Wigmore Street, then a street of dress and antique shops, tea rooms and chiropodists. This was rented from Debenhams and managed by Ted Ould, a future managing director of the company.

From the vantage point of history, we can see that the 1920s were central to the organization of the company. In many ways the foundations were laid for its success at design management and product development 50 years later. In this period, Gordon Russell also honed and refined his own ideas, not only as a designer but as a theorist and propagandist destined to spend a large part of his career trying to persuade other industrialists of the value of good modern design.

It was in the 1920s that he firmly rejected the 'precious' nature of his Arts and Crafts background, yet he never lost sight of its values. His espousal of good industrial design to be produced by machine was bound up in a belief in aesthetic quality – in life and work. It had nothing to do with cynically chasing profits and sending the sales curve shooting upwards, as argued by the American super-stylist Raymond Loewy, who first came to prominence in the late 1920s with an appeal to the baser instincts of clients. To Gordon Russell, Loewy's tactics smacked of low cunning, and he was not impressed by them, even though later on he became friendly with Loewy, Walter Dorwin Teague and other American designers who had belonged to the school of streamlining. To streamline a stationary object, such as cooker or refrigerator, seemed ridiculous to Russell. William Morris may have got it wrong about the relationship between hand and machine but, in another sense, his social strictures continued to resonate through Gordon Russell's life.

Within weeks of the new showroom's opening, that enterprise – and the entire Gordon Russell company with it – was threatened with disaster. The Wall Street Crash had destroyed the market for higher-priced furniture and the lucrative transatlantic trade in antiques, handmade glass and textiles for the American market. As if to make things worse for the Russells, fewer rich Americans stayed at the Lygon Arms. 'The gale swept our little ship from stem to stern,' wrote Gordon Russell in *Designer's Trade*. Help, when it arrived, did so from the unlikeliest of sources.

Chapter 3

1930–1940

MURPHY, MASS PRODUCTION
and MODERNISM

The dawn of a new decade 'did not present a smiling face', according to Gordon Russell. Economic hardship in the early 1930s led to the realization that the only way out of the crisis was to concentrate on selling lower-priced furniture in greater numbers. The trade in expensive luxury items had been all but decimated by the Wall Street Crash, and Gordon Russell's courtship with machine production needed to become a lasting relationship if the company was to survive. The problem, of course, was how to achieve this without sacrificing the commitment to quality on which the company had built its reputation. There was also the question of where to find the customers. At this critical point in 1931, a telephone call to Gordon Russell from an engineer by the name of Frank Murphy changed the company's entire destiny – and influenced the whole course of British industrial design.

This page and opposite: Murphy A8 radio cabinet in plywood and black walnut, designed by Dick Russell, 1932. The collaboration with Murphy opened up new vistas for Gordon Russell Ltd

VOLUME AND QUALITY

Murphy had just started making radio sets and was looking for a better alternative to the radio cabinets currently available from cabinet-makers. Gordon Russell had been recommended to him by the two men who had played such an influential role in the furniture firm's development in the 1920s – Percy Wells and John Gloag. In *Designer's*

Murphy B23
(above) and A72
(opposite) radio
cabinets, designed
by Dick Russell. His
training was ideally
suited to taking the
Broadway factory
into a new era of
mass production.
The spare, modern
look of his designs
was widely imitated

Trade, Gordon Russell describes how Murphy and his aptly named partner Ted Power came down to Broadway to seek help:

> He (Murphy) felt that radio was too complicated: he wanted simpler, better built cabinets which were as good as the sets. 'Look at this', he said to us, producing a portable cabinet, 'it's just a box. No ideas. Ted and I have spent many hours trying to find out how we can keep these ugly knobs out of sight without making them inaccessible but we haven't got anywhere.'

Sets had to be in the dealer's shops well before Christmas and Murphy's own enterprise hung in the balance, as did the future of Gordon Russell Ltd. In a sense the two companies clung together in the early 1930s, united by a common dependence on innovation for survival and success. Gordon Russell and Frank Murphy were both visionaries, leading young, vibrant and little-understood companies through uncharted waters, and they quickly struck up a strong understanding. Dick Russell's training at the Architectural Association, which he never completed, proved crucial. He now possessed a design methodology capable of leading the Broadway factory into a new era of mass production. As Kate Baynes, Gordon's daughter, comments: 'The difference was that while Gordon learnt in the workshop, Dick learnt at the drawing-board. Dick has never received the true recognition he deserved for his work on Murphy radios.'

Although Gordon had virtually stopped designing, he had a large hand in the design of the very first radio cabinet for Murphy. This model was christened the 'Pentonville' by sceptical dealers, because one of its design features was a grill. Murphy's advertising slogan 'Making Wireless Simple' was printed on all its packaging. Dick was responsible for all subsequent designs during the 1930s. These were increasingly characterized by clean lines and purist forms with no adornment or other unnecessary detail. They are now widely recognized as classic designs of the period.

Within a couple of years Dick Russell's designs for Murphy were beginning to influence other manufacturers. Reviewing the annual Radiolympia exhibition in the September 1933 *Gramophone* magazine, writer P Wilson noted: 'Mr Russell has simply swept the board. I should hate to ascribe to him some of the monstrous developments that have been made from his clean lines and simple beauty of form. But even these exaggerations are in their way a tribute to his success.'

The more the radio cabinets distanced themselves from the decorative Cotswolds flavour of the first model, uncluttered by bars, frets or grills, the more they were responsible for introducing a new spare and modern visual language into British industrial design during the 1930s. Though not such a keen devotee as his brother Dick, Gordon Russell was interested in Modern Movement ideas on architecture and design, and during his visit to the celebrated Stockholm Exhibition of 1930, designed by Gunnar Asplund, he had been exposed to the latest in functional Modernism. It was in Stockholm that he also met the legendary Finnish designer Alvar Aalto, whose furniture he later stocked in his London showroom. However, as the architectural historian Nikolaus Pevsner has pointed out, adoption of this new modern style, whether in furniture or radio cabinets, posed problems in production for Gordon Russell Ltd: 'The flush surfaces, the square legs, the exact unmitigated angles partook of the connotations of machine precision which played such a significant part in the modern style of architecture.' (*Studies in Art, Architecture and Design*)

Gordon Russell himself recognized that the hand skills of the old cabinet-makers at Broadway were not precise enough. As he explained in *Designer's Trade*: 'The (Murphy) engineers, accustomed to working in thousands of an inch, laughed at our idea of a tolerance: a sixteenth of an inch was a crevasse to them! They said we must learn to be accurate, wood or no wood.' The experience of producing cabinets for

A Park Royal factory worker polishes a Murphy radio cabinet

The Gordon
Russell factory at
Park Royal, west
London, opened
in 1935. The facade
was designed by
Geoffrey Jellicoe

Murphy revolutionized the working methods of the company. Its tradition of craftsmanship and commitment to quality became wedded to high standards of engineering in wood. All measurements had to be taken from the inside instead of the outside. Along with greater mechanization, the company introduced a scientific precision and consistency of manufacture which have beeen maintained ever since.

For a furniture company to take this route was highly unusual. In his 'Skill' lecture, Gordon Russell recalled how one of his peers reacted to the news:

> My entry into this trade led Ambrose Heal, a good friend of mine and a member of the Arts and Crafts, to ring me up with astonishment and disapproval in his voice to say: 'I hear you are making radio cabinets!' 'Yes', I said, 'a fascinating job. I expect that it may be all that we are remembered by!'

Also unusual was the role of Dick Russell in making an aesthetic input as an industrial designer on a par with and at the same time as electrical, mechanical and production engineers. Each radio set was designed in its entirety both inside and out before tooling began. Frank Murphy had broken the mould. Until the day he turned up at Broadway, the wireless industry norm had been to design a set and then buy in a cabinet from a range of sketches submitted by a woodworking firm. Gordon Russell was not slow to grasp the significance of this: Murphy was a manufacturer using industrial design not as add-on decoration or ornament, but to shape the product's formal qualities. Russell wrote in *Designer's Trade*: 'Good industrial design goes down to the roots – it is never something added at the end.'

It was no surprise that Dick Russell became Murphy Radio's in-house designer in 1936, assisted by Eden Minns, another Architectural Association graduate. In

Below: the first of Dick
Russell's simple, low-cost
bedroom furniture ranges,
Thirty Four, in oak with
laburnum handles, 1934

Left: modern-style
office desk
designed by Dick
Russell in the 1930s

1935, Gordon Russell had opened a new factory at Park Royal in west London to cope with the growing radio production demands. The facade was designed by Geoffrey Jellicoe. At its peak in the late 1930s the factory employed 800 staff and made cabinets for Ekco, Bush, Ultra and Pye as well for Murphy.

The importance of Murphy Radio to the development of Gordon Russell Ltd as a manufacturer in the 1930s cannot be overstated. While the retail trade made losses, radio production kept the company afloat: 40,000 sets of one model alone were manufactured. Company records for 1937 show that Gordon Russell made 200,000 radio cabinets in just one year. Not that the new-style designs were universally popular with the conservative trade and indifferent public. Even Murphy's own dealers and sales staff 'loathed Dick's designs,' according to a letter from C R Casson, Murphy's advertising agent. 'They may be fine design, modern, beautiful', harassed Murphy reps used to argue '. . . but even if they are beautiful they are out of place in the homes of people buying radio sets.' Frank Murphy was evidently unmoved by opposition to his design policy, while Gordon Russell remarked wryly of the episode in his 'Skill' lecture: 'We discovered that the public were greatly interested in the quality of the sets and would even accept a well-designed cabinet if the set was OK. This did not happen with wardrobes which had to be sold neat.'

On the furniture side, things were predictably as problematic as ever for a manufacturer pioneering modern design at a time when reproduction pieces were so popular. In any case, business was generally depressed in the early 1930s. But the Murphy radio work broadened the company's technological horizons. The contract introduced a new mood of flexibility and confidence into the factory and had a profound effect on the type of work taken on subsequently. In fact it was crucial to survival, for the high engineering demands of radio production prepared the ground for the war work of the 1940s when Gordon Russell Ltd, unlike so many other manufacturers, managed to stay in business by making a wide range of military items – from ammunition boxes and Mosquito wing parts to high precision aircraft models for wind-tunnel testing.

THE TALENT TO SURVIVE

The 1930s marked a dynamic tension within Gordon Russell Ltd between two very different cultures in furniture-making. On one side was the cabinet-making tradition epitomized by Shoreditch-trained W H 'Curly' Russell, who became chief designer in 1934 and held the post for the next 35 years. On the other was the modern architectural approach being developed by Dick Russell and his friends from the Architectural Association. In the centre stood Gordon, who clearly embraced the new while always acknowledging his debt to the old. Curly too took on board many of the new AA-inspired ideas in his work.

By the time Dick Russell had moved to London in 1932 – it was deemed convenient to have a director both resident in the capital and close to Murphy

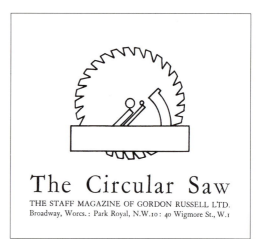

The staff magazine, *The Circular Saw*, which became a lively forum for debate at Gordon Russell Ltd in the late 1930s

Room set made in cherry wood and walnut, designed by W H 'Curly' Russell for the 1937 Paris International Exhibition. Carpet by Marian Pepler

Radio's Welwyn Garden City headquarters – he had already stamped his mark on the company's design direction. The way in which Dick Russell's contribution was integrated into the product development process established an important precedent for British designers, who were increasingly being recognized as a profession in their own right, and had set up their own Society of Industrial Artists and Designers in 1930 (later renamed the Chartered Society of Designers). Gordon always admired his brother and encouraged him, so sharing to some extent a design education he never had. But Gordon also appreciated the value of Curly Russell, who, as his design assistant, had so skilfully interpreted his designs in the 1920s. The international reputation that Gordon Russell Ltd enjoyed in the 1930s was due in no small part to the subtle blend of cultures which brought so many different staff and consultant designers into the company.

The two cultures expressed themselves in the Broadway showrooms just a few yards down from the Lygon Arms. L J Smith, a furniture salesman who joined the company in 1931, recalls how Dick Russell's modern designs were placed at the front of the showroom while a back room was piled high with earlier Gordon Russell designs in the Gimson tradition that could not be sold. These expensive, ornate pieces with ebony and walnut inlays were considered out of date and were sometimes simply given to investors in the company such as William Cadbury or Cecil Pilkington. Yet today it is these very pieces that fetch high prices at auction.

Antiques were still sold at Broadway in the early 1930s, but the trade was so badly hit by the American Depression that Henry Keil, the company's antiques buyer, left Gordon Russell Ltd. Keil later set up on his own business and became famous for antiques in Broadway. According to L J Smith, 'The only Americans who travelled around the Cotswolds in the early 1930s were teachers spending their life savings.' Things got so bad in 1933 that Gordon Russell decided to cut the salaries of all staff, including his own, by 10 per cent. L J Smith remembers that Gordon traded in his car for a small and cramped Austin more in keeping with the austerity of the time. 'The sight of such a big man in that small car was ridiculous,' says L J Smith. 'The steering wheel came up to his knees.'

Despite the economic pressures there were light interludes. When business improved, Gordon rewarded the staff's loyalty and perseverance by sending a group of them, including L J Smith, Curly Russell, R H Bee and Ted Ould, on a cruise for three weeks to study architecture and furniture in northern capitals such as Danzig, Copenhagen and Stockholm. It was evidently a memorable trip, and a characteristically warm gesture on the part of the proprietor. L J Smith recalls that much effort was also put into staff activities. There were football matches between the Broadway and Park Royal factories and large dinners afterwards. Even Gordon Russell himself, who could be a very shy and reserved man, engaged in such antics as imitating a coarse French porter during an office trip to France for the 1937 Paris International Exhibition, where the company was showing a room set designed by Curly Russell and Marian Pepler. It was at the end of the 1930s that

Two contract carpets
designed in 1933 by Marian
Pepler and made by Wilton
Royal. Right: Wood Ash.
Below: Fret, shown in Louis
Fox's West End dress shop

the staff magazine, *The Circular Saw,* became a lively forum for debate.

The Russell family had now become the largest employer in Broadway: when L J Smith started work there in 1931, there were 200 staff in the factory and nearly 20 in the offices and showrooms. Smith remembers being summoned in fear and trembling to Gordon's office on his first day, but Gordon simply wanted to show him the Lygon Arms and buy him a pint of beer. Despite its expansion and mechanization, the enterprise remained very much a family firm. When a blaze in June 1934 gutted ten thatched cottages built for workers at the factory, it was a disaster not just for the company but for the entire area. After the fire was put out, S B Russell wrote to the local paper, describing the many offers of help for the ten homeless families as 'a magnificent triumph of practical sympathy and goodwill by the whole village'.

Dick Russell and Marian Pepler. They married in 1933 and played leading roles in taking the company into the vanguard of European Modernism

In the early days Toni Russell, Gordon's wife, played a leading role in running the showrooms at Broadway, taking responsibility for buying in factored goods such as glass, fabrics, carpets and china to complement the furniture. In October 1933 Marian Pepler, who was based with Dick in London (they married in December) took over the job and became responsible for factored goods in both the Broadway and the 28 Wigmore Street showrooms. Marian had been encouraged by Dick to design rugs and carpets in a new geometric modern style that would complement his furniture and interior designs. Working for such manufacturers as Wilton Royal, Alexander Morton and Tomkinsons, her work swiftly came to public attention. It was commended for its grace and originality, and promoted by Gordon Russell Ltd in its advertising for complete room settings. Her first rug, in 1930, had been called Snowshill, in honour of the village in which Dick Russell's parents lived. When she and Dick Russell designed the Lobden house for Albert Hartley in 1932, four rugs – two circular and two rectangular – were specially designed for the interiors.

During the slump of 1933, the first Gordon Russell showroom, run by Ted Ould at 28 Wigmore Street, was set to close. As the company's financial chief, R H Bee, observed in a sales report, the shop was not attracting passing trade and was only taking orders from existing customers who had previously ordered direct from Broadway. But at that point Dick Russell, who had set up a design studio with Marian Pepler in the basement of the shop, intervened. He argued passionately that the showroom should remain open with key modifications to the retail strategy. In a report to the board, Dick Russell wrote: 'The shop falls between two stools by being neither a specialist decorator dealing exclusively in rather highly priced and precious furniture and furnishings nor a furniture shop with a comprehensive stock at all prices.' His solution was to produce and sell

Gordon Russell Ltd's
40 Wigmore Street
showroom, opened in
1935 and designed by
Geoffrey Jellicoe. The
showroom's modern image
included pale blue neon
fascia lettering

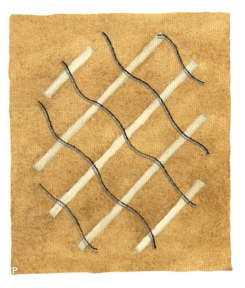

Right: sketch for textile design, Beach, by Marian Pepler, circa 1933. Below: Weston dining-room in oak, a strong seller through the 1930s

GORDON RUSSELL LTD

A SELECTION OF NEW DESIGNS IN
FURNITURE · FABRICS · RUGS

40 WIGMORE STREET, LONDON, W.1, and BROADWAY, WORCS.

Telephones: WELbeck 4144, Broadway 45

Interior of the
showroom,
demonstrating
the dramatically
modern and
uncluttered
display principles
developed by
the company

Late 1930s catalogue for
Gordon Russell Ltd, showing
the range of factored goods
selected by chief buyer
Nikolaus Pevsner

cheaper furniture ranges while at the same time improving the showroom display
to attract a better class of customer. The shop was to feature entire room sets, and
not simply a window display.

The company was now beginning to ride out the storm of the early 1930s.
Sales of rugs, curtains and simple, modern, low-cost unit furniture ranges designed
by Dick Russell were selling well enough to warrant more retail space and Gordon
Russell Ltd began to expand its retail business in the capital. The move to larger
premises at 40 Wigmore Street, again rented from Debenhams, was therefore a
logical conclusion of this upturn. Gordon Russell asked Geoffrey Jellicoe – who
was closely associated with the company throughout the 1930s – to design the
showroom, which had been used by Debenhams as a warehouse. Jellicoe installed
a simple plate glass frontage, lit the fascia lettering with pale blue neon tubes, and
punctuated the 120-foot length of the showroom with a series of indirectly lit
bays. Indeed the entire lighting of the shop was most ingenious and provided a
dramatic illuminated setpiece for late-night audiences leaving the concerts at the
nearby Wigmore Hall. Inside, the sense of modernity was tangible: there was no
counter, and customers could sit on the furniture and touch the textiles. Marian
Pepler's Aquamarine rug took pride of place in the window alongside Dick
Russell's furniture.

The new shop was opened at the end of 1935 with a press and private view.
Ted Ould had been promoted to the board of Gordon Russell Ltd and put in
charge of contracts, so the job of running the London showroom was given
to L J Smith. He recalls that his brief was clear: to sell more of the company's

Marian Pepler's Boomerang
rug (foreground) and Dick
Russell's circular Chastleton
table (centre), displayed at
40 Wigmore Street

factory-made products and make the showroom seem less like a society interior decorator. Geoffrey Jellicoe's showroom design worked superbly to this end. The architect describes it as 'one of the most pleasing projects I've ever done. Gordon had a very clear mind which resulted in a very clear brief. We worked harmoniously together.'

Nikolaus Pevsner, who in *Studies in Art, Architecture and Design* describes Marian Pepler's rug designs as having 'a sensitivity and quiet perfection not surpassed anywhere in Europe', took her place as the company's chief buyer in 1936, shortly after the opening of 40 Wigmore Street. Pevsner had arrived in Britain two years earlier as refugee from the rise of Nazism. He had been forced to give up his job in Dresden Art Gallery but immediately came to Gordon Russell's attention when he undertook a year's research study at Birmingham University into the design of products for British industry. In compiling his survey, Pevsner visited hundreds of manufacturers. The factory at Broadway was one of them. In 1935, when Pevsner gave a lecture on his findings to the Design and Industries Association, Gordon Russell had been in the audience. According to *Designer's Trade*, 'He (Pevsner) showed such a comprehensive grasp of the subject that I went over to Birmingham the next day and asked him if he would like to buy textiles, rugs, glass and so on for us. Although he had never been in business he said he would like to consider it.'

Pevsner worked for Gordon Russell until 1939, when he left to become the assistant editor of the *Architectural Review*, a post which set him on the road to become one of the finest art and architecture critics of the modern age. The fact that such an unusually gifted and well-informed writer should remain with the company for so long reflected Gordon's Russell's ability to attract and retain the brightest young talents in British design. The company was undoubtedly an exciting place to be in the late 1930s and Pevsner expressed an enormous respect and admiration for its achievements in his subsequent writing. Years later, when he was awarded the Gold Medal by the Royal Institute of British Architects in 1967, his celebration dinner was in Broadway as a guest of Gordon Russell.

Immediately after joining the team at 40 Wigmore Street Pevsner added fine German wallpapers and fabrics to the ranges on sale. L J Smith thought it 'absurd that a fellow of Pevsner's knowledge and horizons should be restricted to fabrics', so Pevsner bought in Thonet bentwood chairs from Czechoslovakia as well as furniture by Alvar Aalto and Bruno Mathsson. Jewish refugees from Nazism living in nearby Hampstead were particularly good customers of the new showroom, as were stage folk such as Robert Donat and Charles Laughton. But as the war years drew near, Pevsner's cosmopolitan buying policy came in for criticism from the workforce at Broadway. Not only was the foreign furniture considered unpatriotic, but the construction of some of it ran counter to the best traditions of English cabinet-making. The issue was raised in the April 1939 edition of the staff magazine *The Circular Saw* by two cabinet shop workers, Adriaan Hermsen and

P J Wade: 'Surely the sale of these articles aggravates our own employment problem,' they wrote. Pevsner was requested by editor Val Freeman to answer his critics immediately. He did so with masterful lucidity:

> We don't bend solid beechwood as Thonet's have done for eighty years. Climatic conditions would not, I am told, favour such an industry. The design is good and clear, and the construction sound. We don't bend ply either, at least not in our cabinet shops. Aalto, the Finnish architect, has made a name all over Europe for this particular technique and these logically designed and made shapes . . . As long as such limitations of manufacturing and of style exist in our production – and are they not bound to exist always and everywhere? – I am afraid 95% British is as far as we can go: in furniture that is to say. Fabrics would be quite a different story.

The London showroom remained open until 1940, when, in the words of L J Smith, 'there was nothing left to sell'. The Broadway factory had been turned over to war work and Smith himself was directed to chase payment for defence contracts from government departments. He remembers an unsuccessful visit to the Navy accounts department at Blackheath to see if a Gordon Russell Ltd

40 WIGMORE STREET, W.I

next to the Times Book Club is the address of our new London showrooms. They are much more spacious and attractive than the old premises at 28 Wigmore Street and we hope that you will come and see our interesting display of

NEW FURNITURE, FABRICS AND WALL PAPERS

We shall be pleased to send you a copy of a leaflet illustrating some of our recent work.

GORDON RUSSELL LTD

of BROADWAY, WORCS.   London showrooms: 40 WIGMORE ST., W.I.   Telephone: WELbeck 4144

The products promoted through the new showroom attracted many customers, including refugees from Nazism, who responded positively to Pevsner's buying policy

invoice could be paid. It was a far cry from an earlier engagement with the Navy in 1938 when L J Smith supervised a Gordon Russell contract to furnish the quarters of the King and Queen on board *HMS Repulse*.

Despite its inevitable closure by the time of the Blitz, Gordon Russell's London showroom at 40 Wigmore Street played its full part in the brief flowering of Modernism in Britain in the late 1930s. It was an exciting time for Dick Russell and Marian Pepler, who were then living at the famous Highpoint flats in Highgate designed by Berthold Lubetkin. As standard-bearers for modern design they were very much at the centre of the movement. Their friends included Hugh Casson, Ambrose Heal, Oliver Hill, Misha Black, Wells Coates and F R S Yorke. Gordon Russell's own position was more ambivalent. He was undeniably one of the most active and conspicuous patrons of modern design in Britain, yet, as Marian Pepler explains, 'He stood back from the Modern Movement, aloof from it. He didn't want to embrace it. Essentially he remained a supporter of the Art Workers' Guild.'

Cartoon by Frank Whitton from *The Circular Saw*, alluding to Pevsner's controversial policy of buying some furniture from overseas

THE END OF AN AGE

Although he no longer designed for the company in the 1930s, Gordon Russell's workload remained enormous. In particular his role as an articulate propagandist for good design was developing all the time. Val Freeman remembers accompanying Gordon round the Cotswolds as he gave a series of lectures to local groups, complete with eclectic collection of slides and magic lantern show. One of his lectures was entitled 'There goes a fellow with no curiosity', after a favourite French cartoon of a man remarking on a passing hearse. It was typical of his black humour. On one occasion Gordon had such a heavy cold that Val Freeman offered to take over the lecture – this time on another favourite theme, fitness for purpose. 'You should be able to. You've heard it so many bloody times,' was Gordon's blunt response. It was in those draughty village halls on cold winter nights that Gordon Russell honed his beliefs about design and advanced the arguments that he would carry so forcefully into the international arena in the 1940s.

During this period Gordon was also hard at work on his home at Kingcombe, another anchor which tied him to the Cotswolds throughout his life. It was his fascination with landscape architecture that brought him into contact with the landscape architect Geoffrey Jellicoe, who had authored a number of books on garden design. The relationship lasted throughout the 1930s. Jellicoe remembers his first impression of Gordon Russell's towering presence: 'A rather tall chap wearing a new Homburg hat appeared one day at my door. I must say I was drawn to him. He was very perceptive about what I was trying to do in landscape design.' As well as the garden at Kingcombe and the elevation of the new factory building

OFFICER – CAN YOU DIRECT ME TO THE SHOP OF MY DREAMS?

Concept for an advertisement to promote the London showroom

at Park Royal, Jellicoe's projects for Gordon Russell included a garage at the Broadway works and even a masterplan for the village of Broadway itself, the first of its kind under the new town-planning act. He found Gordon to be a first-rate architectural client:

> Gordon was intensely interested in how the modern world was developing, but at the same time he had one foot in the past. I felt much the same way. Perhaps that's why we had so much sympathy for each other's views. We would often discuss the philosophy of life on walking tours of the Cotswolds.

Jellicoe first visited Kingcombe in 1931 and later submitted a masterplan for the garden with his partner Russell Page. In 1936 Jellicoe's former partner Jock Shepherd, who had been working on the reconstruction of the Shakespeare Theatre at nearby Stratford-upon-Avon, designed an extension to the house, which was by that time straining to accommodate Gordon, Toni and four active young children.

Gordon's attention to detail at Kingcombe became legendary. He would meticulously record all the plants he had purchased in a diary. He bought the fields around Kingcombe so that the family would have uninterrupted views and no neighbours. The house and garden became a showpiece for entertaining. Overseas visitors to the factory at Broadway in the 1930s included the Japanese ceramicist Shoji Hamada, Bernard Leach, Harold Stabler, American industrial designers Walter Dorwin Teague and Gilbert Rhode, and Bauhaus emigrés Walter Gropius and Marcel Breuer. Gordon had joined the community of the world's leading design names and was clearly able to discuss his company's aspirations on equal terms.

Gordon's daughter Kate remembers Kingcombe always being full of visitors, including many from Scandinavia: Gordon was an admirer of Scandinavian design, regarding it as a form of Modernism which had a human face and a continuity of craft tradition. 'Every detail at Kingcombe was agonized over,' says Kate. 'But the pursuit of beauty exacted a price on the family.' Indeed it cannot have been easy for the Russell children to grow up with such a stern father whose interest in aesthetic quality was all-encompassing – or for Toni Russell to keep a large house and growing family in line.

In a sense Gordon was simply passing on to his own children elements of the tough, demanding childhood he had spent under the ever-watchful eye of his father. In January 1938, S B Russell died – on the thirty-fourth anniversary of taking over the Lygon Arms at Broadway. An English oak coffin was designed and made in the factory, and his body was taken in an open farm wagon strewn with

The Cave Man restaurant
at Cheddar Gorge, with
furniture designed by Curly
Russell, 1934. Geoffrey
Jellicoe and Russell Page
were the architects for the
scheme

Room set for a *New Designs from Gordon Russell* brochure (see opposite). New graphic styles such as this (by Frank Whitton) reflected the company's concern for creative experiment in the late 1930s

daffodils from Snowshill, where he had lived, to Campden seven miles away, where he was buried. When Gordon Russell rewrote his autobiography not long before his own death, he described his father in unsentimental terms as:

> . . . the main early influence on my life because he was a good talker and was always willing to talk in a way that could be understood by children. He was of a sensitive and imaginative disposition, with a tendency to take life too seriously, caused partly perhaps by starting work too early and working too hard. He worried a good deal and was not altogether easy to live with.

S B Russell did, however, mellow in later life and devoted much time to church activities and working with prisoners released from the jail at Gloucester. Marian Pepler remembers him as: 'a remarkable man, a collector of fine glass and pewter, a lover of good architecture. He was a strong aesthetic influence on Gordon'.

Gordon described his father's death as 'the end of an age'. In 1939 storm clouds were gathering in more ways than one. Many of Gordon Russell's initiatives, including the formation in 1938 of the Good Furnishing Group comprising a body of like-minded retailers, were soon cut short by war. Design had been given its head within the company during the 1930s but, as trading conditions deteriorated rapidly, the company's financial affairs began to unravel. Minutes of board meetings in the late 1930s are littered with talk of 'crisis' and 'desperate measures'.

Gordon's strong streak of idealism meant that, like his father before him, he was not able to balance compromises in technical quality and visual standards against the need to survive financially. In the July 1940 edition of *The Circular Saw*, he wrote under the heading 'Great Britain versus Boche and Wops':

> The Directors wish to make clear that they are reducing the two retail shops and turning over to still more war work as rapidly as possible. Don't be impatient. Even with the present spurt there is not a vast amount of war woodwork, and some of the other work we are doing such as radio is of national importance.

But three months later he was forced to resign as managing director of the company. The bank was threatening to withdraw support if R H Bee was not appointed in his place to run Gordon Russell Ltd.

Gordon retired to his garden at Kingcombe in October 1940 and never again held an executive position in the company. He had been managing director for just seven years (having taken over from his father in 1933) but in that short time he had established an international reputation for the Broadway factory. According to Trevor Chinn, who replaced Curly Russell as chief designer at Gordon Russell Ltd in 1969 and held the post until 1986, the success of the company in the 1930s was 'due to the strong mix of in-house and external designers working

Leicester City Electricity
Showrooms, a 1934 contract
scheme featuring Marian
Pepler's Aquamarine carpet

together. An ethos developed which continues today'. Trevor Chinn joined the company in 1938 as a 14-year-old apprentice. On his first day he was taken in to see Gordon who told him: 'Don't be frightened. I felt exactly the same on my first day at work.' Gordon Russell had, of course, started work for his father at almost the same age.

Autumn 1940 did not only mark the withdrawal of Gordon Russell from the company. On the night of the German raid on Coventry, a stray incendiary bomb from a German war plane landed on the great barn at Broadway that Gordon had drawn so lovingly as a boy. The thatched roof immediately caught fire. Inside, stockpiles of fine furniture and textiles brought from London for safe storage were destroyed. Amongst the furniture was ironically a large order for Sir John Anderson, Minister for Air Raid Precautions. Trevor Chinn remembers cycling into the factory on the night of the blaze to rescue drawings from the drawing office. These were taken away to a local inn for safe keeping. Up on the hill above Broadway, an ack-ack brigade who took regular baths at the Lygon Arms thought the hotel was on fire so rushed down to help, thinking they were about to lose their bathing facilities. Gordon, who had joined the Special Police for the second time, saw the fire as symbolic: 'Our world was indeed disintegrating,' he wrote later.

At Kingcombe, now nearly 50, Gordon Russell had only his stonecutting, beekeeping, planting and reading to occupy him. Yet within two years he had been given a new national role which enabled him to bring his unique skills to bear in the general effort to win the war and prepare for peace.

Chapter 4

1941–1959

A PUBLIC LIFE *on*
THE NATIONAL STAGE

With the Broadway furniture factory given over entirely to war work and its founder no longer in executive control of his company, Gordon Russell could have been forgiven for thinking that he had withdrawn from the vanguard of modern design for good. As he busied himself in his garden at Kingcombe, he must have felt that the pioneering days of the late 1930s had been a mirage. Yet, as the supply of timber became more erratic in the early 1940s and air raids destroyed more homes and furnishings, the threat of a 'furniture famine' contrived to bring him back into the limelight in a role of national significance.

This page and opposite: Utility chairs, produced in the early 1940s. Gordon Russell saw in war-time furniture shortages an opportunity to wean the British away from the pre-1939 pseudo-Victorian tradition

USING AUSTERITY TO ADVANTAGE

In 1942 Gordon Russell received an invitation from the socialist Hugh Dalton, just appointed president of the Board of Trade by Winston Churchill, to join the Utility Furniture Advisory Committee. The committee was made up of designers, manufacturers, government spokesmen and consumers. Dalton pressed upon them the serious need for state-controlled production of domestic furniture, given the escalating war damage. Any designs had to take into account the acute shortages of skilled labour and raw materials such as plywood, steel, cellulose and textiles as well as timber. Gordon Russell immediately saw a chance to break

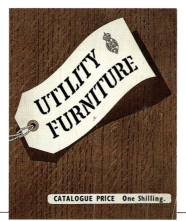

CATALOGUE PRICE One Shilling.

The first Utility furniture catalogue, which went on sale on 1 January 1943: designs, by H J Cutler and Edwin Clinch, were deliberately made easy for a range of manufacturers to follow. The furniture was simple and functional, as shown below and opposite

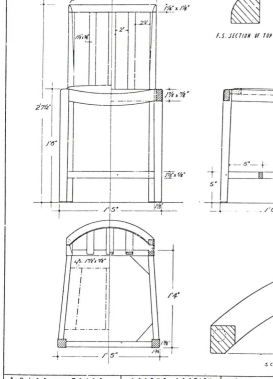

F.S. SECTION OF TOP

| BOARD of TRADE UTILITY FURNITURE | SECOND SECTION LIVING-ROOM | MODEL NO. 3A. OCT: 1942. | DINING |

Furniture for an Alternative

LIVING ROOM

with the pre-1939, pseudo-Victorian tradition of reproduction furniture and use the austerity and production constraints of war-time Britain to introduce a less ornate, more honest and modern style of furniture. He energetically threw himself into the work of the Utility furniture committee, arguing that modern design was the proper – and only – interpretation of Dalton's demand for 'pleasant furniture' which would be economical to produce and robust in performance. As Russell explained in *Designer's Trade*:

> The basic rightness of contemporary design won the day, for there wasn't enough timber for bulbous legs or enough labour for even the cheapest carving and straightforward, common-sense lines were both efficient and economical. It was an acid test and, naturally, some diehards only admitted the result reluctantly. It must have been a bit of a shock that a type of design which had been pioneered for years by a small minority – whilst the trade looked on and laughed – should prove its mettle in a national emergency, but so it was, to the amusement of some and to the amazement of others.

The plan was to limit furniture production to just a handful of state-approved designs and prohibit all other furniture. Gordon Russell admitted: 'That's pretty drastic if you like, but needs must when the devil drives.' In fact, he could scarcely contain his excitement at this heaven-sent opportunity to re-educate public taste, which he felt would be more receptive to Modernist ideals than the conservative retail trade. The committee, chaired by Sir Charles Tennyson, commissioned nine designers to submit ideas and chose the work of two, H J Cutler and Edwin Clinch, both from High Wycombe, to create the first Utility furniture range.

Cutler and Clinch worked in a simple, concise, workmanlike idiom, and were careful to explain their designs with a precision that left novice manufacturers in no doubt as to their intentions. Their approach proved well suited to the unusual circumstances: Britain's mass-production furniture factories, such as Gordon Russell Ltd, were all taken up with high priority military contracts, so the makers of Utility furniture were local woodworking firms, many with no furniture experience whatsoever. Because of transport difficulties, the idea was to make Utility stock in the areas where it would be sold and used. As many as 700 different firms took part in the exercise. Orders to make the new furniture were accompanied with a warning of heavy penalties for shoddy workmanship.

The first exhibition of Utility furniture opened at the Building Centre in London in October 1942. Gordon Russell viewed it with satisfaction, describing it as 'a step in the right direction'. He was also perversely encouraged by the attacks from all sides: the furniture trade considered the range too advanced and the *Architect's Journal* called it 'very ugly'. But the reception from the popular press was generally warm, even if the use of hardboard for backs and drawer bottoms prompted headlines about furniture made of cardboard. When the range went on

sale on 1 January 1943, exempt from purchase tax, the Board of Trade was effectively introducing a new national style in furniture design. Only newly-weds and households 'bombed out' by the war were eligible to buy the furniture, using coupons. Hugh Dalton expressed his regret that he did not qualify.

Gordon Russell now had the bit between his teeth and was not about to let go. He started to consider whether the Utility specification, which he had played a central role in establishing, could provide the basis for a quality mark in the post-war period once controls had been lifted. He studied ways in which the drastic implementation of simple, modern furniture design could be consolidated so that the clock could never be turned back to the vestiges of Victorian excess. More research was needed, so he suggested to the Board of Trade that the Utility Furniture Advisory Committee should set up a Design Panel to explore solutions in the longer term. In his own memoirs Russell seems genuinely surprised to be made chairman of this panel, but it could be that he brilliantly engineered the opportunity, showing an ability to manipulate the political establishment that rarely deserted him.

Certainly Gordon Russell relished the prospect of putting together a design team of his own choice, although unfortunately he could not call on Dick Russell: his brother had joined the Royal Navy to work in its camouflage unit. The work of the Design Panel focused on two possible scenarios: one a worsening situation (with intensification of bombing destroying all conventional production facilities);

Filling in the coupons for Utility furniture. Only newly weds and bombed-out families were eligible, much to the regret of Hugh Dalton, president of the Board of Trade, who wished he could qualify

and the other an improvement (with many scarce materials coming back into circulation). Gordon Russell's research took him from one government department to another, and out into the streets of the East End to talk to consumers. He deliberated with a number of the outstanding artists and designers of the day, including Henry Moore and the Czech architect Jacques Groag, an assistant of Adolf Loos, who had described ornament as a crime. Meanwhile the designers Cutler and Clinch were retained to provide the bedrock of the Utility look. This, as many commentators have pointed out, has now assumed the status of a period classic. It is a style which embodies all the virtues of good, practical, well-made furniture but is strangely out of place in the English design tradition of patterns rather than pure form.

Utility Cotswold armchair. Each Utility range was named after a region in England

Using government controls to his own advantage, Gordon Russell was now going through another period of change. He was spending a great deal of time away from Kingcombe in war-torn London, although he never spent a single night in a bomb shelter. His World War One experiences had, he remarked, given him a 'hatred of dugouts and pillboxes'. His work with the Design Panel of the Utility committee kept him close to the centre of power, so that when the first discussions on the formation of a Council of Industrial Design were held, he became a vigorous participant in them.

Early plans for the Council centred on the need to expand exports once the war was over, and this depended on improved standards of industrial design. Prime mover in setting up a national body to coordinate and promote this campaign was Sir Thomas Barlow, head of the leading Lancashire textile firm Barlow & Jones, who was then director-general of Civilian Clothing at the Board of Trade. In the 1930s Barlow had set up a design research unit within his company under textile designer Marianne Straub, a progressive and unusual move. Gordon Russell held him in the highest esteem, describing him as 'an altogether remarkable man'. Barlow was appointed the first chairman of the Council of Industrial Design (later to become the Design Council) and S C Leslie, a civil servant from the Ministry for Home Security, its first Director. With Europe still ablaze, the Council held its first meeting in December 1944. Its brief was succinct: 'To promote by all practicable means the improvement of design in the products of British industry'. As designer, manufacturer and propagandist, Gordon Russell was, of course, uniquely equipped to carry out the Council's brief and was invited to be one of its 24 founder members. Within three years he would be its Director.

By the end of the war in 1945, Gordon Russell had gathered a strong Utility team around him on the Design Panel. Many of the names were familiar from his

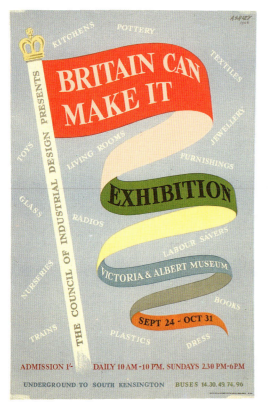

KITCHENS POTTERY

BRITAIN CAN MAKE IT

TEXTILES

THE COUNCIL OF INDUSTRIAL DESIGN PRESENTS

TOYS LIVING ROOMS JEWELLERY

GLASS FURNISHINGS

RADIOS

NURSERIES EXHIBITION

LABOUR SAVERS

VICTORIA & ALBERT MUSEUM

BOOKS

TRAINS SEPT 24 - OCT 31

PLASTICS DRESS

ADMISSION 1/-   DAILY 10 AM -10 P.M. SUNDAYS 2.30 PM-6PM

UNDERGROUND TO SOUTH KENSINGTON   BUSES 14.30.49.74.96

Poster designed by
Ashley Havinden
for the 1946
'Britain Can Make
It' exhibition, in
which Gordon
Russell played a
leading role

furniture company in the 1930s and included Dick
Russell, Eden Minns and Robert Goodden. Both
Gordon and Dick Russell were now Royal Designers
for Industry, Gordon having been elected in 1940 and
Dick four years later – the only two brothers to share
the distinction at that time. A new generation of Utility
designers took over the mantle of Clinch and Cutler and,
encouraged by the reappearance of scarce materials, set
about meeting public needs with a refined modern style.

In 1945 the election of the first post-war Labour
government filled many people with the hope of a better
future, Gordon Russell amongst them. He may have
become a wealthy industrialist and landowner but
he hardly came from a 'county' background. After
all, he had experienced something of a working-class
upbringing, albeit a highly unconventional and
aesthetic one; he had also left school at 14 with no
formal qualifications and served in World War One
in the ranks. For all his love of the fine things in life,
he harboured some socialist leanings. Gordon Russell
Ltd had been founded on the ideal of making decent
furniture for ordinary people at a price they could
afford, and according to Val Freeman, 'Gordon had leveller tendencies.' Russell's
commitment to the Utility furniture programme was also inspired by more than
the basic desire to dictate functionalism to the masses. Certainly, once the war was
over, he appeared committed to serving a Labour administration.

In November 1948 restrictions were lifted and manufacturers were given more
freedom to produce their own furniture designs. But continuing shortages of some
materials meant that the basic Utility principles – precursors to 'green' policies in
their emphasis on saving energy and resources – were still valid. It was not until
the early 1950s that the programme stopped completely.

Utility is linked in the national psyche with the 1946 'Britain Can Make It'
exhibition. Gordon Russell played a leading role in both. The idea for a morale-
boosting exhibition to show people what they might hope to buy again after years
of austerity was proposed in 1945 by Sir Stafford Cripps, the new president of
the Board of Trade. The proposal for a national exhibition landed on the desk
of S C Leslie, the Director of the Council of Industrial Design, within 24 hours
of Cripps' appointment to the Board of Trade. Leslie's staff suggested the name
'Britain Can Make It' because it evoked the war-time slogan 'Britain Can Take
It'. As a Council member, Gordon Russell swiftly moved to the heart of things.
James Gardner, whose war-time exploits in camouflage (including inflatable
rubber tanks to fool the enemy) had become legendary, was appointed designer

of the exhibition, and Basil Spence chosen as its main consulting architect. Russell arranged for L J Smith, who had run the company's London showroom before the war, to return from the Air Force and take charge of the designers working on the exhibition. 'It sent me grey,' recalls L J Smith. 'I had to organize 26 different architects, each designing a different room.'

'Britain Can Make It' opened at the Victoria and Albert Museum in September 1946. Crowds thronged to see the displays of goods, all of which had been vetted by a selection committee. Poorly designed products had been rejected, much to the dismay and anger of some manufacturers. As many as one and a half million people are estimated to have attended, despite the one shilling entrance fee. Naturally, Gordon Russell Ltd took a stand at the exhibition as part of managing director R H Bee's concerted drive to get Broadway back into making and selling fine furniture after years of producing aircraft parts and ammunition boxes.

By now Gordon Russell was sitting on a number of influential government committees, including one looking into design in the furniture trade and another examining how to improve design standards in purchases by the Ministry of Works. When S C Leslie was recalled to the Treasury by Sir Stafford Cripps, there was a certain inevitability in the invitation from Sir William Barlow for Gordon Russell to take up the post of Director of the Council of Industrial Design. According to Russell's memoirs, several other candidates had applied but were considered unsuitable. He himself deliberated over whether to accept:

> There was only a small group which thought a Council of Industrial Design a good idea, the majority regarding it as a waste of money . . . no country had set up such a body and backed it with an adequate government grant. There were people in the Treasury and the Board of Trade who argued that public money ought not to be spent on such a project.

1950s ornate reproduction furniture of the type Gordon Russell despised and fought against. Despite his efforts some manufacturers continued to produce these styles

A wide range of better grade Dining Sets from 45½ Gns. or 9/- weekly

Gordon Russell nevertheless decided to take on the challenge and started at the Council in September 1947.

REBUILDING A REPUTATION

While Gordon Russell himself was in London playing a new role on the national stage, his company at Broadway was stoically and resourcefully adapting to wartime shortages under the leadership of R H Bee. The engineering discipline and precision instilled by the Murphy radio production proved useful for government defence contracts. Bill Ould, who joined his brother Ted Ould in the company in March 1941, recalls how the firm made thousands of model aircraft to assist civil defence ack-ack brigades in recognizing enemy planes. Just two months later he was sent to close down the Park Royal factory in London, so ending an extraordinary chapter in the company's history.

Times were often hard during the war and, as Bill Ould recalls, 'we all had to work like hell'. By this time women made up half of the workforce at Gordon Russell Ltd. As soon as it was free of war work, the company joined the Utility furniture-making programme. It had missed the first contracts in 1943, but now it swiftly made its presence felt in government circles. Many substantial orders would later come from official bodies such as the Ministry of Works, the Property Services Agency and the Department of the Environment. Utility furniture was becoming increasingly popular with the public. Bill Ould believes that it helped to establish a strong retail market for Gordon Russell Ltd in the post-war years.

After the war there were also new beginnings for the Lygon Arms. Douglas Barrington, an Australian serviceman befriended by Don Russell, was appointed manager of the hotel at the end of the hostilities. He had no civilian clothes and remembers serving drinks in the evenings still wearing his naval officer's uniform. Barrington, the son Don Russell never had, became a director of the hotel a year later, and in 1956 its managing director. After Don's death in 1970, Barrington inherited Don's majority share in the Lygon Arms. According to Barrington, Gordon Russell never appeared to resent his steady progress in becoming an intimate of the Russell family, sharing in their success and observing the complex web of family relationships. 'There was a powerful streak of integrity in the Russells,' says Barrington. 'Of course, they had flaws and frailties, but that was what made them endearing to so many people.'

Much revolved around Mrs S B Russell, who lived at the hotel after her husband's death and remained a powerful presence right up to her own death in 1956. Revising his autobiography late in life, Gordon described how fortunate he had been as a child that 'my mother came from farming stock, had a placid temperament and took things just as they came without trouble or fuss.' This common-sense approach contrasted with the more imaginative and volatile ways of his father. When Mrs S B Russell first came to the Lygon in 1904, she had demanded a half bottle of champagne every evening after serving the guests: it

The Birmingham office of Hardy Spicer, with Gordon Russell reception furniture. The scheme was designed by Dick Russell's architectural practice in 1958

was the only way she could get through the grind of constantly renovating the place. After 1940 she was able to live as a guest in the hotel, although she had to sign for her champagne: Douglas Barrington made all the Russells sign for their drinks in the Lygon. His rule caused a stink but introduced the financial control previously lacking.

At the factory, meanwhile, the production of Utility furniture led to a strong emphasis on furniture for the retail trade. As competitors were beginning to

1953–54 interior for Murphy Radio advertising agents, C R Casson: Dick Russell's practice employed the unique skills of Gordon Russell's Broadway factory for the project

emulate its designs, Gordon Russell Ltd decided to move upmarket with larger, more expensive room suites targeting the upper middle class customer. The company's long-established reputation for quality had survived the upheavals of war, and orders flowed in from major retailers such as Heal's, Harrods, Liberty's, Bowman's of Camden Town and Dunn's of Bromley. This was a golden era for retail sales, a boom time when customers might have to wait eight weeks for orders to be made up in the factory. Designer Trevor Chinn remembers manning the company stand at an Earl's Court furniture show in the early 1950s: the throng of visitors was so great that salesmen had to stand on chairs handing out leaflets over the heads of the surging crowd.

The work of Curly Russell, then chief designer, and Dick Russell, who had returned from war service to resume private practice in 1946, figure strongly in this period. But the retail successes enjoyed by the company in the late 1940s and early 1950s (when retail orders represented 80 per cent of all sales) were not to be sustained. By the 1960s many independent furniture retailers had been forced out of business or swallowed up by chains. Furniture salesmanship was no longer viewed with the respect it once commanded and courses for salesmen organized by Gordon Russell Ltd failed to stop the rot. Many at Broadway wanted the company to abandon the retail market long before it eventually withdrew in 1972. In a sense it maintained its position in the retail trade out of deference to Gordon himself, who remained committed to selling good design to the general public.

The pressures of retailing certainly took their toll on the company's design standards in the 1950s: conservative demands from buyers stifled the innovation of the pre-war years and it was a period of financial consolidation with modest profits rather than bold gambling on creative experiments. With Gordon Russell occupied with affairs of state at the Council of Industrial Design, Don Russell was chairman of the company. In 1950, on R H Bee's death, Ted Ould became managing director, later followed by his brother Bill.

The company's hallmarks of quality, innovation, design and craftsmanship were, however, plainly evident throughout another strand of post-war activity. The contract side of the business began to come into its own as retail sales gradually diminished. A separate contracts company, Russell Furnishings, was established in London in 1946 with L J Smith, R H Bee, Ted Ould and Gordon Russell Ltd each holding 25 per cent of the equity. From the mid-1950s this venture, renamed Gordon Russell Contracts, had an impressive showroom at Stratford Place in London, complete with original Adam ceilings. Gordon Russell Ltd swiftly plugged into the post-war demand for new furniture for universities, schools, hospitals, hotels, churches and other public buildings.

Architects working on these contract projects were intrigued by the Broadway

Dick Russell at his desk at the Royal College of Art. As Professor of Wood, Metal and Plastics, he moved his own practice into the college so that students could witness how a professional design business operated

environment and admired Gordon Russell's own achievements. In the 1950s the culture and ethos of Gordon Russell Ltd became increasingly attractive to them as they redefined the first heroic phase of Modernism. Leading architects such as William Whitfield, Leslie Martin and, later, Arne Jacobsen collaborated successfully with the company on major international contracts. Architect Ray Leigh remembers what it was like to work with the Broadway factory as a young designer. Leigh had joined Dick Russell's practice in 1952 straight from the Architectural Association, where he had trained. He was working on an office interior for the advertising agents C R Casson (of 1930s Murphy Radio fame) when he first made contact with the manufacturer:

> My first impression was that this was an amazing resource for architects. The people at the factory were full of skills and advice, and they loved working with designers from outside. You could come down to Broadway and soak up the atmosphere. It was all about quality and service. If you said to the drawing office 'I don't think this can be done', they would immediately gear themselves up to prove you wrong.

As a partner in Dick Russell's practice in the 1950s and 1960s, Ray Leigh gained a unique insight not only into the workings of the furniture company but also into the private world of the Russell family. This stood him in good stead when he succeeded Bill Ould in 1971 as managing director of Gordon Russell Ltd, the first recognized designer to occupy the post since Gordon himself.

The furniture company leaned heavily on Dick Russell's expertise in the postwar years. Indeed Dick's hand was evident in many of its finest achievements and most prestigious commissions, including a range of furniture for King Feisal of Iraq (who was assassinated before the pieces were delivered) and an English walnut presentation table given to President Eisenhower by the Queen on a Royal visit to America in 1957. Dick Russell's practice worked with Marian Pepler on a new wing for the Grosvenor House Hotel in London, furnishing 92 bedrooms and two suites in a modern style (see page 96), and also carried out three commissions to upgrade the Lygon Arms. This work included building a new dining-room, the Russell Room, in 1958, and involved all three Russell brothers in one project: Don was the client, Dick the architect and Gordon the craftsman, contributing a stone-carved panel to set in the doorway (see page 97).

By the time Dick Russell had designed the simple, classic English oak chair which went into Coventry Cathedral in 1960, and subsequently into other places of worship all over the world, his skill and vision – complemented by the strong in-house design team at Broadway – had gone a long way towards re-establishing and enhancing the international reputation of Gordon Russell Ltd.

Part of a range of furniture designed by Dick Russell for King Feisal of Iraq. The table is inlaid with ivory, pear wood, ebony and silver

Left: classic oak chairs designed for Coventry Cathedral by Dick Russell and made by Gordon Russell Ltd, 1960. Architect Basil Spence commissioned 2,000 at a cost of six pounds each

Left: walnut table replicating President Eisenhower's 1944 D-day landing plans; designed by Dick Russell and presented to Eisenhower by the Queen in 1957

Above: C R Casson offices. The scheme gave architect Ray Leigh his first opportunity to work with the Gordon Russell factory creating custom furniture

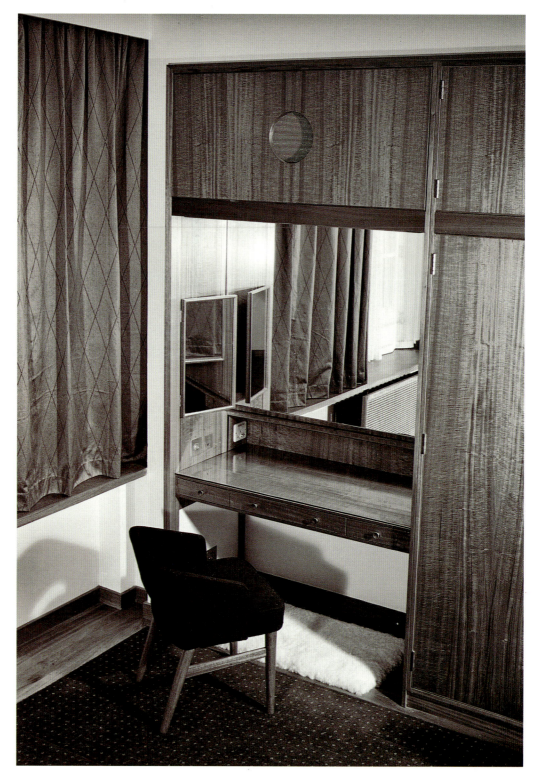

One of the 92 bedrooms
designed for the Grosvenor
House Hotel in 1958 by
Dick Russell's practice with
Marian Pepler

The Russell brothers, (from
left) Gordon, Don and Dick,
celebrating the opening of
the Russell Room at the
Lygon Arms, 1958: it was
the last project on which
all three collaborated

Below: stone
panel carved by
Gordon Russell,
demonstrating
one of his many
craft skills

Gordon Russell
with Paul Reilly,
his successor at
the Council of
Industrial Design,
where Reilly took
over the uphill task
of promoting good
design to British
industry

THE GREAT CRUSADE

In 1948 Dick Russell was appointed Professor of Wood, Metals and Plastics in the School of Furniture Design at the Royal College of Art. At the same time his close colleague Robert Goodden, with whom he had worked at Broadway and on Utility furniture, was appointed Professor of Silversmithing, Jewellery and Glass. Following the tradition, Dick Russell moved his practice into the RCA from 1950 to 1955, so that students could see how a professional design studio operated. Afterwards he continued to work professionally in nearby Jay Mews.

Gordon Russell was already a friend of the RCA's new principal, Robin Darwin, who had applied for the post at his suggestion and had been given the task of revitalizing the college in 1947 so that a new generation of industrial designers could be trained to aid Britain's export drive. Naturally, close links were formed between the RCA and the Council of Industrial Design, with the Russell brothers at the centre. As Gordon explained in *Designer's Trade*, 'It was the Council's job to persuade industry to employ more highly trained designers which the reorganization of the college would provide.'

Gordon Russell recognized that education would need to be at the core of his Council agenda, but, as he remarked years later in his 'Skill' address,

> I don't believe that the Board of Trade really appreciated that the Design Council had an immense education job to do . . . It became pretty clear to me that we should not make a great deal of headway in improving design standards until the Ministry of Education took much more interest in visual education. That meant that the training of teachers should not be solely literary, so that in God's good time they and their students would take some notice of the surroundings in which they lived and worked.

In this Russell was prefiguring moves by the Council 30 years later to influence the content of primary and secondary education. Unlike the Council in later years, he never had funds to tackle the education issue head on. Russell also recognized that industrialists, who naturally resented any kind of government interference or controls, needed to be won over. Hand-in-hand with this was convincing the retailers, and finally the buying public, for Russell knew that converting buyers would bring additional pressure to bear on manufacturers and retailers.

Using these basic premises as his starting-point, Gordon Russell drafted a development report for the Council in the serenity of Kew Gardens and set about his task with characteristic energy. In 1947 he coordinated a programme of Design Weeks all over the country to bring the various industrial, retail and educational interest groups together. Around that time, he was returning from New York on board the *Queen Elizabeth I* when he met a young English design journalist called Paul Reilly, who had been working in America on the editorial staff of the magazine *Modern Plastics*. So impressed was Russell with Reilly's grasp of Council issues that he invited him to join as head of the information division. Reilly swiftly became an indispensable ally and succeeded Gordon Russell as Director in 1960.

The Russell-Reilly axis between the late 1940s and 1970s marked a crusading period for the Design Council, as it became known. According to Keith Grant, who succeeded Reilly as Director in 1977,

> Russell and Reilly were extremely clever at preaching the message and putting design on the map in an opportunistic way. Only after their time were the resources put in place by government to take matters in hand properly.

One of their earliest initiatives was the launch in January 1949 of the Council's own magazine, *Design*. This was a controversial step, as it clashed with a privately run publication, *Art and Industry*. One influential Council member, Sir Francis Meynell, felt so strongly about it that he resigned. The title of the magazine had been suggested by Robin Darwin of the RCA, and Reilly was its leader writer. The cover and logo of the first issue were designed by Robert Harling. *Design* has continued to publish ever since and discussions about the Council's role as a magazine publisher continue to this day.

The launch of the magazine provided an insight into Gordon Russell's management style as Director. Paul Reilly recalled in his own autobiography, *An Eye on Design*:

> The first year of *Design* was the excuse for the first of the innumerable little notes that I received from Gordon Russell throughout the twelve years for which I worked for him, all written in his marvellously clear handwriting and all phrased to enchant their recipient. The first one read: 'At the end of *Design's* first year I write to its competent midwife to say how well I think the child is coming on. As you know I have always believed in it and in the early days had a good deal of criticism both inside and outside the Council which I didn't pass on as I felt so much of it was not constructive'.

Many Council staff who worked for Gordon Russell commented on his ability to get the best out of people by appreciating their work without interfering in it. He was always more interested in broad policy than detail, a patrician figure who spent his weekends at Kingcombe, returning to

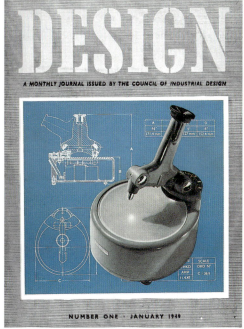

The first issue of *Design*: a controversial move into publishing for the Council of Industrial Design

Above: the Lion and Unicorn Building, designed for the 1951 Festival of Britain by Dick Russell and Robert Goodden. Right: a Gordon Russell Ltd room set from a 1950s Earl's Court exhibition, with bedroom furniture by David Booth

London during the week to stay at the Arts Club and bang the drum for the Council's activities at innumerable public functions. Russell is remembered as a convincing speaker if the audience was willing to be convinced. But when the audience appeared unsympathetic to his arguments, he swiftly lost patience. Reilly recalls the constant uphill battle in promoting good design to British industry:

> Gordon Russell and I invited the directors of the Co-op furniture factory to come and see the difference between their furniture and the furniture being made by Swedish and Danish cooperative movements. We had all the catalogues laid out for comparison, but our guests could not see the difference. (*An Eye on Design*)

In 1951, in a bid to quicken the pace of change in the design of British-made goods, the Government decided to rerun the Great Exhibition of 1851. Harold Wilson, then president of the Board of Trade, conveyed the news to Gordon Russell at the Council. A site for the 'Festival of Britain' was chosen on London's South Bank. Russell argued successfully for the Council to retain some design control over the entire event instead of over just one industrial design pavilion. With Hugh Casson as master planner coordinating the work of many architects and designers, the Council set about compiling a Design Review of industrial products. Russell coordinated a mammoth trawl of industry, instructing his team to select products to strict criteria to avoid enraging rejected manufacturers. The result was a collection of 10,000 industrial exhibits, ranging from tableware and garden tools to locomotives, loaned from 3,500 different firms.

The optimistic and progressive tone of the Festival of Britain filled Gordon Russell with hope that at last the Council had turned the corner in the campaign to improve design and architecture in Britain. He felt sure that the Festival would be the catalyst for a series of important government-sponsored developments to consolidate the first fragile advance. But at the end of 1951, the Government changed. The Tories came to power and failed to seize the initiative. 'The Tories viewed the Festival as Herbert Morrison's plaything and left the design profession high and dry', Keith Grant remembers. 'Gordon was extremely disillusioned by the lack of follow-through.'

In many ways the Festival of Britain marked a turning-point for Russell. He lost faith in political will and appeared drained by his constant brushes with the Board of Trade, or 'Bored With Trade' as he called it. In his remaining years at the Council, staff noted that he would never be drawn on his political convictions. Russell was not alone in his despair: Terence Conran, who worked on the Festival of Britain as a young designer and drew inspiration from Russell in his subsequent entrepreneurial career, also remembers feeling a sense of betrayal.

Despite the setback, Gordon Russell was not about to give up the struggle and in one key aspect he was eventually to enjoy success – the establishment of a permanent national exhibition centre for the Council in central London. The

Visitors flocked to the Design Centre after its opening in April 1956: the showcase (below) swiftly became a model for design centres elsewhere in the world

growing volume of products from British industry and increasing complexity of the specifying process were cited as reasons to open a Design Centre, together with the need to demonstrate new developments to the public. Russell's tireless pronouncements on the subject were instrumental in getting the scheme funded. He was by now a powerful public figure, knighted in the New Year's Honours List of 1955 (following a CBE in 1947). Kate, his daughter, remembers the effect that having a well-known father had on her as a schoolgirl: 'I thought the letters G R on red postboxes stood for Gordon Russell.' She also recalls being taken out of class by the headmistress of her private school and paraded in front of the parents of a prospective pupil as the daughter of a great man.

When visiting her father in London, Kate would accompany him on trips to inspect suitable buildings for the Design Centre. Eventually the ideal site was found at 28 Haymarket near Piccadilly Circus. A new steel and glass facade was designed by Neville Ward, and the Design Centre was officially opened by the Duke of Edinburgh in April 1956. It quickly attracted a stream of visitors from all over the world and consolidated the Council's strong international reputation. The Design Centre became the fountainhead of a host of new initiatives and a model for many design centres in other countries. Sir Gordon himself assumed the role of international ambassador, visiting Russia, Canada and Sierra Leone in quick succession. His influence in Britain ranged from the design of postage stamps to design policy at the newly nationalized British Rail. He was, however, nearing retirement age and, as a director of the Lygon Arms and Gordon Russell Ltd, he did not need to rely on his Council salary. Late in 1957 he decided to start handing over to his successor Paul Reilly (later Lord Reilly), and when he retired fully at the end of 1959, Russell did so with the knowledge that for its work the Council had been awarded one of the most prestigious of all international design awards, the *Compasso D'Oro*.

Russell's contribution to the establishment and development of the Design Council was enormous. His legacy lives on to this day, although Reilly and subsequent Directors have gradually added a harder technological edge to his Arts and Crafts flavoured approach to industrial design. At the end of a unique 17-year stint of public service stretching from war-time Utility and the Festival of Britain to the new Design Centre, Russell returned to Kingcombe, itching to work again on his garden and start his own design consultancy. He left London with much well-earned praise ringing in his ears, but his contribution to design was far from over.

Gordon Russell with daughter Kate at Kingcombe. Together they inspected prospective buildings to house the Design Centre

Chapter 5

1960–1980

THE RETURN *to* CREATIVE ROOTS

Gordon Russell's return to the Cotswolds brought him closer
to his furniture company, in which he had not been actively
involved for 20 years, and to his own design roots. Kingcombe itself
was a haven: in the large and unusual private gardens he had created
in the hills above Chipping Campden, Russell was able to recharge his
creative batteries and reflect on the
different turns his career had taken.
In many ways his 12 years at the
helm of the Council of Industrial
Design had marked the culmination
of his life's work. There had been a
symmetry in the pattern of events,
as Pevsner, a frequent visitor to
Kingcombe during Russell's
retirement years, pointed out:

This page and
opposite: a desk
from the Sycamore
range of office
furniture, designed
by Ray Leigh and
manufactured by
Gordon Russell
Ltd

Making the best furniture by hand, making the best modern
furniture by hand, selling the best modern fabrics and other
furnishings with it, making the best-designed modern furniture
by machine, selling through others, designing modern furniture
on a national scale, and so in the end directing a whole national
movement towards good modern design – no personal
development could be more logical and more satisfying.
(*Studies in Art, Architecture and Design*)

Gordon Russell receiving the Royal Society of Arts Albert Gold Medal for 'services to industrial design' from HRH The Duke of Edinburgh in 1962

However, Gordon Russell still saw a role for himself as an adviser on design policy to large industrial groups. He established his own consultancy at Kingcombe with the help of his secretary from the Council, Rosamund Hogg, who left London to live in Chipping Campden. Clients clamoured for his services, including the Bank of England, which wanted advice on the design of bank notes, and British Rail, whose design problems ranged from rolling stock to teaspoons. At Paul Reilly's request, Russell also went on a lecture tour of 34 English public schools, including Eton, Harrow and Winchester. Reilly's aim was to interest future captains of industry in the value of design. The tour's success convinced him that the Council should concentrate more fully on education in schools in addition to working with industrialists – a policy substantially developed by Director Keith Grant during the 1980s with new awards schemes and publications.

In 1962 Gordon Russell was invited by the Art Workers' Guild to become its Master, and was also awarded the Albert Gold Medal by the Royal Society of Arts for 'services to industrial design'. The recipient the previous year had been Bauhaus founder Walter Gropius. These accolades marked the start of a great many honours bestowed on Russell in the final years of his life. Also in 1962, he travelled to India to advise the government on setting up four schools of industrial design. In two months he travelled 8,000 miles round the Indian continent. His retirement was turning out to be a characteristically unconventional one.

IN THE KINGDOM OF KINGCOMBE

Writing now took up a lot of Gordon Russell's time. In 1964 he published an illustrated book, *Looking at Furniture,* and then went on to complete his memoirs, a task begun in 1944. His autobiography, *Designer's Trade,* was published in May 1968, a vivid and forthright account of a designer's life which was read with interest by many young practitioners. In the same month his son Oliver died tragically. The twin events were in some way symbolic: behind the glittering public life, problems in the family, particularly of mental illness, dogged Gordon Russell. His published memoirs are revealing only in so far as they portray a man who kept the psychological torments of his private life well hidden. His autobiography devotes little or no space to his children, other than to record their births. Gordon Russell had responded positively to the tough, austere upbringing to which his father had subjected him, but his own sons, growing up in a very different age, perhaps reacted less favourably to such distancing treatment. He was, however, closer to his daughter Kate, his youngest child, and very tender and

At home with his
favourite craft objects:
at his Kingcombe retreat
Gordon Russell was able
to recharge his creative
batteries

Above: the vaulted concrete wall at Kingcombe, for which Gordon Russell used hundreds of empty wine bottles from the Lygon Arms. Right: 'G R & T (Toni) 1961' – an example of his decorative engraving work

attentive towards his grandchildren. He spent much time and effort at Kingcombe building a special folly and hideaway for Kate's two children.

In the early 1960s Kate Russell went to Zurich to work on the editorial team of *Graphis* magazine where she met the design teacher, writer and practitioner Ken Baynes. They subsequently married and set up a consultancy together, and both were close to Gordon Russell during his retirement years at Kingcombe. They recognized the value of his work and set about documenting it. Baynes' own pioneering work in design education in a sense picked up where Gordon had left off at the Design Council and was the subject for animated discussion between the two men.

Gordon Russell, of course, could hold forth on a great many subjects. He was a voracious reader with an extraordinary factual and visual memory. At one particular Arts Club dinner a group of colleagues tried to catch him out by deliberately bringing the conversation round to the origin of bows and arrows, having studied the subject in advance. But Gordon dug into his deep fund of knowledge to astound them all with fresh information. On another occasion a seventeenth-century John Nibb clock was stolen from the Lygon Arms: Russell drew an accurate picture of it for the police from memory. His encyclopaedic grasp of how the material world worked extended right down to the size of the different paving stones on the streets of London.

In other respects he was very unworldly. When invited to appear on the radio programme *Desert Island Discs* he had difficulty bringing to mind ten records that he had even listened to, never mind wanted to take with him to a desert island. Japanese clients of Gordon Russell Ltd presented him at different times with a radio and camera, but neither really interested him. Until he became very ill with motor neurone disease just two years before he died, he never even had a television set. When one was finally installed he watched the *Last Night of the Proms* and was astounded that young people were interested in classical music.

There was an austerity and other-worldliness about the life Gordon and Toni Russell shared at Kingcombe. The house was full of Gordon's favourite craft objects but the couple enjoyed little in the way of conventional material comforts. However, in keeping with the finest traditions of the pioneers of the Lygon Arms, they knew how to entertain well and did so frequently. Kingcombe positively hummed with visitors. Once a diffident and shy man, Gordon was now famous for the warmth of his hospitality. Among regular guests were the engineer Sir Ove Arup, the Hungarian-born textile designer Tibor Reich, whose textile mill at nearby Stratford-upon-Avon supplied Gordon Russell Ltd, and the Design Council Director Keith Grant, who particularly valued Gordon's lucid insights into Civil Service problems.

Gordon Russell was a great connoisseur of food and wine, and in particular a lover of fine madeira and port. According to his daughter Kate, he always said there was no situation in life that could not be improved by a good meal. One of

Hard at work
painting a wall
at Kingcombe:
in landscape
architecture
Russell saw
the broader
environmental
view that he
thought all
architects and
designers
should take

his favourite expressions was 'succulent morsel'. Whilst at the Council, he had
put Paul Reilly's problems of ill health down to eating sandwiches at his desk.
But despite the largesse with which he and Toni Russell entertained visitors,
most of his money was spent on Kingcombe's constantly sculpted and caressed
garden landscape, an increasingly elaborate labyrinth of arches, avenues, ponds,
canals, water tables, hedges and secret corners. Russell was fascinated by landscape
architecture, seeing in it the broader environmental view that he felt all architects

and designers should take. He built up an extensive library of gardening books and became an Honorary Associate of the Landscape Institute. Rewriting his memoirs just before his death, he speculated on the comparison between landscape design and furniture manufacture: 'In dealing with industrial products it is possible to visualize and make a mock-up of the final fixed form. This is far from being the case in landscape work where trees, shrubs and plants all alter in shape, size and colour from month to month and year to year.'

Gordon Russell was so forceful and resourceful in begging, borrowing and stealing materials for his garden that his brothers nicknamed him 'the jackdaw'. On one occasion he wrote to Dr Beeching, who was at the time axing rural railway stations, to ask for some long stone platform slabs for a new garden construction. On another occasion, he instructed the storeman at the Lygon Arms to send up to Kingcombe every empty bottle of wine. The bottles were needed for building a vaulted concrete wall alongside a canal (see page 108). The storeman remarked: 'It must be the first time Sir Gordon has ever asked for an *empty* bottle of wine.' It was not unknown for Gordon to intervene during renovations at the Lygon to inquire if newly dug topsoil could be transported up to his garden, or even to provide the local stationmaster with jam jars to collect ferns for him around the railway tracks.

Kingcombe was Gordon Russell's Utopia. It was altogether a consuming passion, one which must at times have infuriated his family and friends, but one which held a key to his personality. According to Ken Baynes, 'Gordon's most distinguishing characteristic was his single-mindedness. He had an extraordinary determination to pursue his vision. It gave him great strength, but in the case of Kingcombe, perhaps it damaged others'. Building work never relented. Toni Russell had to endure perpetual change in her home just as Mrs S B Russell had had to live under the dustsheets amid the constant renovations and extensions in the Lygon Arms. It is clear that without Toni's support, Gordon Russell could not have achieved all he did. She was an unfailing tower of strength throughout his life and although opposed to some of the more fanciful ideas at Kingcombe, she invariably gave way. 'It can't have been easy for her at times,' Ken Baynes reflects. 'She had a very independent mind and elegantly ferocious sense of humour.'

Single-mindedness was an attribute shared by all three Russell brothers to varying degrees. They also shared a sense of not quite being part of the modern world while clearly making a contribution to its advance. Their attitude to money provided an insight into the rarified atmosphere that they inhabited. Despite the business empire founded by their father, Gordon had no insurance and was unrealistic in his views on what it cost to run Kingcombe; Don insisted on living in rented accommodation when he left the Lygon Arms, and refused to buy his own house despite his position as a leading hotelier; and Dick's architectural practice was often financially stretched despite the glowing reputation of its principal. What they all shared was an unwillingness to compromise on quality:

Early 1960s contract schemes: a new bedroom wing at the Lygon Arms, Broadway (right) designed by Dick Russell's architectural practice; and St Catherine's College, Oxford (below), designed by Danish architect Arne Jacobsen

everything had to be exactly right, whatever the cost to themselves or others. The Russell brothers were big men in every way, physically strong and tall (Gordon the tallest at six foot three) with a certain aura about them, and powerful in the contributions they made in their respective fields.

In March 1968, the Duke of Edinburgh paid an official visit to Broadway to look round the furniture company and enjoy the pleasures of the Lygon Arms. Gordon Russell Ltd had been granted the Royal Warrant in 1939 by Queen Elizabeth (the Queen Mother) and in 1961 by Queen Elizabeth II. The Duke's own interest in industrial design had been stimulated by his friendship with Gordon Russell in the early years of the Council of Industrial Design. This was an important family occasion for the Russell brothers, and the last time they were all present on such an auspicious occasion.

DOVETAILING WITH MARKET DEMANDS

The 1960s brought mixed fortunes to Gordon Russell Ltd. The pressures of competitive pricing in its two main markets – domestic retail and local authority contracts – increasingly dulled the cutting edge of its design policy. Under the pragmatic leadership of the Ould brothers, the company for a time made financial stability a higher priority than innovation, in contrast to Gordon's pioneering pre-war days. But there were highlights – including, most notably, the collaboration with the Danish master architect Arne Jacobsen on furniture for St Catherine's College, Oxford – and architects and designers continued to hold the company in high esteem.

The company's corporate identity turns over a new leaf for the 1960s

However, standards in the retail market were generally worsening and looked as though they could drag Gordon Russell Ltd down with them. In 1967 the board decided to take remedial action and appoint a director of design to upgrade design standards and initiate new product development. Architect Ray Leigh, who had worked with Dick Russell since 1950, was ideally suited to the job. He had worked extensively with the factory on contracts and on a number of renovations at the Lygon Arms. Above all, he understood the culture of the company and its founder. The job appealed to Leigh because, as he explains, 'As an architect, you are always in the hands of those who build or make. Here was an opportunity to control the manufacturing process totally. If the end results were poor, there would be nobody to blame but yourself.'

After interview by Ted and Bill Ould, Gordon Russell and Douglas Barrington, Ray Leigh was given the post. It was an important move for the company and signalled a dramatic change in its design fortunes. Shortly after Leigh started as design director at Broadway, Gordon became chairman in place of Don Russell, who died in 1970. This change marked the start of a design renaissance within the company which gathered pace when Ray Leigh assumed total control as managing director early in 1971 and continued after Gordon Russell's death.

It was a tough assignment for Ray Leigh, as an architect, to take over full

The Heritage range
(right), designed by
Robert Heritage,
and the Group 3
domestic furniture
range (below)
designed by Ray
Leigh, Trevor Chinn
and Martin Hall:
some of the last
domestic furniture
produced by the
company

responsibility for a manufacturing company without having any comparable management experience. But the enterprise had been founded by a designer and built on a commitment to design, so the choice of an Architectural Association graduate to lead the company was in every way appropriate. In 1969, Gordon Russell Ltd made its swansong in the retail market: Ray Leigh, Trevor Chinn and Martin Hall designed an innovative range of domestic furniture, entitled Group 3, and the company also commissioned work from designer Robert Heritage. But a year later the decision was made to pull out of this market altogether. 'Gordon was saddened by this,' says Leigh, ' but he was also a realist and recognized the shortcomings of retailing. A company of our size could not compete seriously in both the retail and contract markets.' At the same time, Gordon Russell Contracts, formerly known as Russell Furnishings in Stratford Place, London, closed with the retirement of L J Smith. It was the end of one era and the start of a new one as the contracts division reverted to Broadway under the direction of Laurie Wolder.

Architect Ray Leigh, appointed by Gordon Russell Ltd to revive a sense of design excellence within the company

The 1970s saw an expansion in the company's design activity and its range of business. Ray Leigh saw a lot of Gordon Russell during this period:

> Gordon was very interested in the direction the company was taking, and he had the ability to support and encourage initiatives even if he found the designs we were developing excessively modern. He was never critical of what we tried to do, as long as we stuck to our principles. And as he had encountered every kind of technical, financial and human problem at Broadway in the twenties and thirties, he was able to put my own problems into perspective.

Leigh fostered a creative atmosphere which recalled the heroic days of the 1930s: in-house designers and consultants collaborated to produce the best results; craft skills unique to Broadway and handed down from generation to generation were used within a fresh contemporary context; and *Dovetails*, a successor to the pre-war staff magazine *The Circular Saw*, was introduced. The company exhibited regularly in France, Germany, Italy, America and Japan. Its products were also manufactured under licence in the Far East following an agreement with the Seibu Group of Japan.

Many of the newly introduced pieces were Ray Leigh's own designs. Dick Russell, Leigh's mentor, also contributed some office designs, and remained partly involved in the company right up until his death in 1983. Other members of the design team made a significant contribution to the company's development, most notably chief designer Trevor Chinn, who worked with Leigh on a number of

The 1970s marked a deliberate shift of company policy towards the office sector. Above: Series 1 range, designed in 1970 by Ray Leigh and Trevor Chinn. Below: Series 90 designed by Ray Leigh in 1977

Above: Broadway 2 office furniture designed by Ray Leigh and Trevor Chinn in 1974. Left: Series 45 boardroom table designed by Trevor Chinn in 1979

A range of furniture
commissioned from Jorgen
Kastholm in 1979, as part of
the company's attempt to
enter the German market

ranges and was also a key influence in catalogue, exhibition and showroom design. In a career that stretched from the late 1930s to 1986, Chinn became a pivotal figure in the company's design fortunes. He remains an authority on the firm's history.

Martin Hall, chief designer of Gordon Russell Contracts, was another important figure during this period. He handled the work associated with the total contract furnishing service offered to architect, design and end-user clients, as well as contributing to standard ranges. In developing the contract market so successfully, Gordon Russell Ltd was demonstrating the same opportunism and flexibility of spirit that it had shown in its early history, when it had moved from antiques into modern design, from hand into machine production, from furniture into radio cabinets, from war-time production into Utility and then into retail, embracing each new opportunity as it arose.

Rosewood veneer conference table designed by Martin Hall during a period when the company began to apply traditional craft skills in a new creative context

By 1979, the company was enjoying such a strong international reputation that it made serious attempts to enter the German and American markets by commissioning ranges from Dusseldorf-based designer Jorgen Kastholm and leading US architects Skidmore Owings and Merrill. That year, the company was one of four organizations to be given a Presidential Award for Design Management by the Royal Society of Arts. The other recipients were W H Smith, Lucas Industries and JCB, all far larger companies. The award, presented by the Duke of Edinburgh, was a measure of how far Gordon Russell Ltd had progressed during the 1970s. Happily, the firm's founder was still around to see it happen.

PICKING UP THE THREADS

At Kingcombe, Gordon Russell was designing furniture for the first time since 1930. The sudden reactivation of his personal design skills just three years before his death was one of the more extraordinary aspects of his life. What made him start designing again nearly 50 years after he had stopped so abruptly?

The catalyst for the change was the retirement in 1977 of Adriaan Hermsen, the Dutch-born works manager of Gordon Russell Ltd, a stalwart who had been with the company since 1928 and was a great admirer of Gordon. For some time Russell had been looking for the opportunity to test out his ideas on the relationship between hand and machine production. He was unhappy with the sterility of much modern furniture and regarded it as having negative tendencies. In Adriaan Hermsen he at last had an expert craftsman on hand to interpret his rudimentary sketches and produce his designs. The two men happily joined forces and spent many long hours working together.

The collaboration began when Gordon Russell needed a new dining-table for Kingcombe. He purchased a quantity of yew timber from a local tree surgeon and with it designed the first of several pieces which also included a dressing table, stool and workbox for Toni Russell, a twelve-sided table, drawing-room table and clock case. The pieces combined hand and machine techniques and reflected the desire to create decorated furniture with sound functional qualities. The style was traditional, but in no way were the pieces reproductions: they had a sophistication and authenticity all of their own. In their book, *Gordon Russell*, Ken and Kate Baynes remark of the dining-table, 'This was the moment to show decisively that the bigotry of the Arts and Crafts Movement against the machine was as damaging as the bigotry of the Bauhaus against decoration.' Ray Leigh, meanwhile, finds the furniture exceptional for the way in which 'Gordon just picked up where he had left off at the end of the 1920s. It was almost as though the intervening years of Modernism hadn't happened. If anything, the pieces were more ornate and decorative than before.'

The return to designing represented Gordon Russell's practical demonstration of his belief that hand and machine could be unified in furniture-making. Despite the mechanization of industry, he never overlooked the importance of handwork. While Director of the Council of Industrial Design, Russell had insisted that the Design Centre should exhibit a few craft pieces free of charge, and in retirement he became a founder member of the Crafts Advisory Committee, playing a key role in bringing the Crafts Council (which the Committee later became) and the COID close together. Ironically Russell's new pieces emerged exactly when his original furniture from the 1920s was beginning to fetch high prices at Sotheby auctions, a development he viewed with great pride and interest.

In November 1978, when Gordon Russell was invited to make the annual address to the Faculty of the Royal Designers for Industry at the Royal Society of Arts, he chose the lecture title 'Skill' to encompass the debate on the relationship between hand and machine work. He was already very ill, suffering from gradual paralysis of his muscles, a cruel fate for such a physical man, and needed assistance from his daughter Kate in turning the pages of his text. But all the good and the great of British design turned out to hear him speak. This is how he concluded the lecture:

> The Arts and Crafts Movement scorned the machine. The Modern Movement which followed it imagined the machine would solve all our problems. Both are regarded with some suspicion today. No country could benefit more than ours from taking a searching, objective look at production as a whole. I agree so wholeheartedly with Dr Schumacher that one of the most fateful errors of our age is the belief that 'the problem of production' has been solved.

Gordon Russell's vision of the future was bound up in the pursuit of quality, whether attained by hand or machine:

Picking up from the 1920s: a workbox (left) in yew and laburnum designed by Gordon Russell for his wife Toni and made by Adriaan Hermsen. The small tray is for a glass of sherry. Below: large yew-tree table combining hand and machine techniques

Occasional table designed by Gordon Russell – another piece from his 'retirement' years at Kingcombe

I look forward to the time when every factory will have a small hand unit which would not only be valuable for making prototypes but would teach young people far more of the materials they will use than they can learn at present . . . Don't forget that hand and machine are complementary – an improvement in one leads in time to an improvement in the other and, as William Morris noted nearly a hundred years ago, any improvement in the work men do leads rapidly and inevitably to an improvement in the men who do it.

Even at the end of his life, Russell was still influenced by the Arts and Crafts line of William Morris. Indeed there have been many comparisons drawn between the two design pioneers. Both were men of vision and courage. Both were gifted and prolific in their work at different times in their lives. Both created something entirely new on which others were able to build. Neither were particularly good businessmen: Russell was always determined to achieve his aims whatever the cost. But whereas Morris articulated clear political beliefs, Russell's own views in the years after the 1951 Festival of Britain were increasingly hard to discern. In the view of Ken Baynes, with whom he often discussed politics:

Gordon was a High Tory of the school which sees great value in the contribution of the working classes. He greatly opposed state intervention in people's lives, but he certainly wasn't a snob. He didn't value people for their position but for what they did and thought. He was extremely sceptical of the value of many people in high places.

Gordon Russell had a traditional view of British life in which everyone had their place and their own defined contribution to make. 'Although he admired dry-stone wallers in the Cotswolds, he didn't think they should be running the local council,' explains Ken Baynes. 'In that sense he wasn't an egalitarian.'

Russell himself recognized the oddball nature of his personality. In the epilogue to his autobiography, he wrote: 'I am a bit of a nuisance. I can't be neatly docketed and put in the right pigeonhole. I have friends of all sorts and all ages.' He did, however, express humanitarian and environmental ideas which were in many ways ahead of his time. Around the time of the first successful NASA moonshot he wrote: 'The technological changes which are taking place at an ever-increasing pace have not, unfortunately, been balanced by a corresponding growth in humanities . . . Is it really so much more important to make a slum of the moon than to abolish our slums?'

According to Sir Terence Conran, Gordon Russell was 'one of those peculiarly English geniuses who are not given the full recognition they deserve'. Gordon Russell furniture was made for Bryanston, where Conran went to school, and the Festival of Britain was both an important point in Russell's career and the start of Conran's. The founder of Habitat and patron of the Design Museum regards Russell's work as a major influence on the direction he has taken. There are many uncanny parallels between the two men's work: in the furniture they have designed, the books they have written, their entrepreneurship and retailing, their mutual interest in the Arts and Crafts Movement, and their commitment to design education. Even the Lygon Arms evokes the restaurants Conran enjoys running, and both men, of course, had connections with Heal's. Conran recalls that Russell's outbursts about the state of furniture retailing struck a chord when he opened his first Habitat store in 1964. Russell in turn admired the style of furniture Conran produced and sold. If there is, as many have suggested, a direct link between William Morris and Terence Conran, then Gordon Russell more than anyone provides that link.

An Enduring Legacy

Gordon Russell's last two years were punctuated by the struggle against his debilitating illness and his growing frustration that he could not find a publisher willing to take his re-edited memoirs, *A Designer's Education*. A proposed retrospective of his work at the Victoria and Albert Museum was cancelled and he despaired that he had failed to make much progress in putting his cherished views across. 'The job is like pushing a tank uphill,' he wrote. However, Russell's contribution was not ignored. In July 1980 he received an Honorary Doctorate from the Royal College of Art in the garden at Kingcombe, and in October that year the Design Council magazine, *Design*, featured an interview of him by editor James Woudhuysen. It proved that Russell could still comment with great insight on contemporary affairs despite being unable even to use his hands. In the month the interview was published Gordon Russell died, at the age of 88. By a strange coincidence, it was the Director of the Design Council, Keith Grant who drew up in the drive at Kingcombe just 30 minutes after Gordon Russell's death on 7 October 1980. Russell was buried in St James the Great Church at Chipping Campden. His wife Toni died within the year.

Gordon Russell's obituary in *The Times* occupied more column inches than the one for John Lennon, who also died that autumn. John Gloag, who had done so much to encourage his early work in the 1920s, wrote of Russell in the *Architectural Review*: 'Despite his great achievements and well-deserved fame, he remained a modest, almost diffident character; but his judicious reticence masked an alert and unforgettably original mind.'

Gordon Russell as Ray Leigh
remembers him. The portrait,
by Carel Weight, hangs in the
company's Broadway offices

Throughout his life, Gordon Russell's great skill was making connections: between hand and machine, craft and design, theory and practice, and landscape and architecture. He built bridges between the history of furniture and new trends, private industry and state policy, local traditions and national movements, and British design and international markets. His work as a designer encapsulated the twentieth century, spanning two world wars, the rise and demise of Modernism, consumer booms and depressions, and the growth of mass communications, transport and marketing. His contribution – from design and manufacture to writing and lecturing – touched on all these aspects and they in turn touched him. As an unrivalled international ambassador for British design, he could study the Shakers in America or visit Aalto in Scandinavia, yet he remained a Cotswolds countryman at heart, rooted to the place his family chose to make their home in 1904.

In his obituary, John Gloag described Gordon Russell as having 'a perceptive awareness of country skills and crafts; not the hothouse artificiality of the arty-crafty revivalists, but the innate sympathy and understanding of materials and methods'. That of course made his own furniture and that of his company so essentially English. During the 1980s, when a glut of matt-black-and-chrome designer objects dominated, it was all too easy to overlook Russell's contribution. His well-mannered and timeless work seemed out of tune with the breathless tenor of the times. But now, as more enduring and environmental values assert themselves, Gordon Russell can again be placed in a proper perspective, which recognizes the classic virtues of honest design, superb craftsmanship, quality detailing and the influence of good design on the human spirit. The continued survival and strength of the company that bears his name is testament to the permanence of his ideas.

Tables from
the Thesis range
of executive
boardroom
furniture designed
by Adrian Stokes
in 1986

GORDON RUSSELL FURNITURE TODAY

Six years after Gordon Russell's death – and more than 80 years after the Russells first arrived in the Cotswolds village of Broadway by horse and trap – the two Russell family businesses on the main street passed out of the family's hands. The furniture company Gordon Russell Ltd was sold to chair-maker Giroflex in June 1986 for £3 million. A month later, in an uncanny parallel, the Lygon Arms was sold to the Savoy Group for £4.7 million. The financial gamble taken by Gordon Russell's father back in 1904 had paid handsome returns. Both new owners made commitments to preserve the unique character and reputation for quality that the furniture-making and hotel businesses had enjoyed during the years when the Russell family was in control.

In the case of Gordon Russell Ltd, the name was earmarked to achieve even wider fame. Giroflex owners Chester Wedgewood and Jeremy Simpson floated their enlarged furniture company on the London Stock Exchange in November 1986, renaming the group Gordon Russell plc to capitalize on one of the most respected and evocative names in British design. They both admired the design legacy of Gordon Russell and in particular the Broadway factory's supreme skills in manipulating materials.

By the time of the sale, architect and designer Ray Leigh was chairman of Gordon Russell Ltd. In 1982 the board had appointed Chris Whittard and Laurie Wolder, both already directors and key figures in running the company, as joint managing directors. Whittard

Above: office group by
Henry Long, winner of
the first prize in the
company's international
design competition organized
with *Architectural Review* and
the Design Council in 1984.
Right: table by Gerard Taylor,
third prize winner.

took responsibility for finance and production, whilst Wolder continued to be responsible for sales and for negotiating prestigious contracts, at home and abroad.

This new arrangement gave Ray Leigh more time to concentrate on design and product development. In 1984 he organized an international design competition with *Architectural Review* and the Design Council which attracted more than 120 entries from 17 countries. Fittingly, the judges included Terence Conran, furniture designer Ron Carter, once a consultant for Gordon Russell, architect James Stirling, Jane Priestman and Ray Leigh himself. The quality of design thinking, demonstrated by the three main prize-winners, Henry Long, Maurice Holland and Gerard Taylor, reflected the essence of a refined English Modernism that Gordon Russell himself worked to achieve during his lifetime.

Once Gordon Russell Furniture became a public company under Chester Wedgewood's aegis, the commitment to innovation was reinforced. From 1986 onwards British furniture designer Adrian Stokes was commissioned to create several new ranges of furniture for the company. His reaction was typical of the attitude of a new generation of young designers towards Gordon Russell: 'There was a sense of awe about the company. With its quality, history and record of achievement, it was a manufacturer of genuine stature and I discovered fantastic skills in the factory.' Prior to developing products for the company, Adrian Stokes had read Gordon Russell's autobiography, *Designer's Trade*: 'He was really a pioneer of modern methods rather than craft methods. In our furniture we tried to innovate in a way we hope he would have respected.'

At the end of the 1980s, as a global business recession loomed and the international contract furniture industry was characterized by a frenzy of mergers and acquisitions, Gordon Russell plc was in turn taken over by multinational company Steelcase Strafor, Europe's market leader in office furniture. Employing over 5,000 staff in Europe and with a European turnover in excess of £300 million, Steelcase Strafor has the global resources to invest in the research and development necessary to create office design solutions for the 1990s and beyond.

According to Edward Cory, chief executive of Steelcase Strafor and Gordon Russell's new chairman, the multinational decided to buy the Gordon Russell company for three key reasons. The acquisition increased the group's manufacturing capability in the UK and effectively doubled the size of its business in the British market. It also introduced Gordon Russell's expertise in wood craftsmanship and manufacture to a group best known for its steel products.

Edward Cory has been concerned to revitalize and promote the Gordon Russell brand name as a separate entity with its own unique history and culture, and separate management. In moves

Below: desk by Maurice Holland, second prize winner in the *Architectural Review* competition

Axis conference
table and desk,
designed by Adrian
Stokes

which brought the company's pioneering traditions up to date, Ray Leigh was recalled to the Gordon Russell board and Neil Brown, a former works manager at Broadway, appointed managing director. Edward Cory explains:

> If you look at Gordon Russell's heritage, it is one of entrepreneurship, international vision and innovation. It is not about old men in white coats caressing wood. The company is far more than just a grand relic from the past, an Austin or Morris in the car industry. The heritage can be made accessible and relevant to contemporary markets without the company losing that special quality, style and mystique.

Steelcase Strafor divides the international office furniture market into three segments: systems furniture; freestanding furniture; and high-design, high-image furniture. Edward Cory sees Gordon Russell Furniture as having the capability to succeed in the second and third categories. 'It is a design leader, an innovator in terms of materials and it has strong British roots which have wide appeal,' he comments. 'It has the image in furniture of Aquascutum or Burberry in fashion.' Steelcase Strafor has made a speciality of buying companies with a strong national identity and distinguished design pedigree. Gordon Russell is in good company alongside Cassina of Italy and Artifort of Holland, which augurs well for the policy of promoting certain individual quality brands in furniture.

A dormant period in product development ended with the production of a new Gordon Russell executive desking range to coincide with the centenary of Gordon Russell's birth on 20 May 1992. Gordon Russell product development manager, Mino Vernaschi, describes how the range, designed by consultants Gerard Taylor and Daniel Weil, follows the best company traditions: 'Gerard Taylor has worked very closely with the people in the factory in the same way that Gordon Russell worked at the bench with his craftsmen to create his early designs. Also, there are echoes of Utility in the stringent costing for production and economical use of materials.' A further link with the past is provided by Daniel Weil's role as Professor of Industrial Design at the Royal College of Art, an institution closely connected with both Gordon and Dick Russell.

The new range includes two different variants to suit different market sectors, and deliberately utilizes the unique wealth of construction and finishing skills at Broadway. Future Gordon Russell products will be demonstrating those skills on the surface, not hiding them away, says Mino Vernaschi: 'It is really all about detailing, adding value where it can be seen and appreciated, and taking out cost where it can't be perceived. In a sense the company is going full circle.'

Edward Cory's intention is not to treat Gordon Russell like a museum but to make the company a progressive force in the future. As the Cotswolds company gears up for a new chapter in its history on the occasion of Gordon Russell's centenary, these are sentiments that the founder – an unsentimental believer in the march of progress – would surely endorse.

Bibliography

BOOKS

Allwood, Rosamund and Laurie, Kedrun, *R D Russell Marian Pepler*, London, Inner London Education Authority (1983)

Baynes, Ken and Kate *Gordon Russell*, London, The Design Council (1980)

Pevsner, Nikolaus *Studies in Art, Architecture and Design*, London, Thames & Hudson (1982)

Reilly, Paul *An Eye on Design*, London, Max Reinhardt (1987)

Russell, Gordon *Designer's Trade*, London, George Allen & Unwin (1968)

Russell, Gordon *Looking at Furniture*, London, Lund Humphries (1964)

MAGAZINE ARTICLES

Dover, Harriet 'Utility Days' *Telegraph Magazine*, London (2 November, 1991)

Eliahoo, Rebecca 'Gordon Russell's Lasting Qualities', *Designers' Journal*, London, Maxwell Business Publications (November, 1984)

Gloag, John 'Gordon Russell and Cotswold Craftsmanship', *The Architects' Journal*, London, EMAP Business Publications (15 August, 1928)

Gloag, John, Obituary of Gordon Russell, *The Architectural Review*, London, Maxwell Business Publications (November, 1980)

Leigh, Ray 'Design Management', *Royal Society of Arts Journal*, London, RSA (May, 1980)

Russell, Gordon 'New Ideas in Furniture', *The Listener*, London (7 March, 1946)

Russell, Gordon 'Skill', *Annual Address to The Faculty of Royal Designers for Industry* at The Royal Society of Arts, London, RSA (1 November, 1978)

'S B W', 'Modern Furniture and Glass', *The Studio*, London (May, 1927)

Walker, Christine 'Four Dab Hands at Design Management', *Design*, London, The Design Council (December, 1979)

Wells, Percy 'Gordon Russell', *The Architects' Journal*, London, EMAP Business Publications, (20 and 27 January, 1926)

Woudhuysen, James 'Beginning at the Bench', *Design*, London, The Design Council (October, 1980)

UNPUBLISHED AND PRIVATELY PUBLISHED TEXTS

Channon, Anne *R D Russell Designer for Industry* 1930–35, Royal College of Art thesis (1984)

Leake, Graham *Gordon Russell: Decent Furniture for Ordinary People*, Birmingham Polytechnic thesis (1983)

Naylor, Gillian *A History of Gordon Russell 1904–1976*, Broadway, Gordon Russell Ltd (1976)

Ould, Bill *Quality in Furniture: Retail Furnishers' Course*, Broadway, Gordon Russell Ltd (1957)

Russell family, *The Story of An Old English Hostelry*, published privately (circa 1910)

Russell, Gordon *A Designer's Education*, unpublished autobiography (1979)

Russell, Gordon *Honesty and The Crafts*, published privately (1923)

Index

A

Aalto, Alvar 59, 73, 74, 125
Adams, Katherine 26
Alexander Morton (carpet manufacturers) 67
Allsopp, Samuel & Sons 11
Anderson, Mary 27
Anderson, Sir John 81
architects 44, 49, 52, 76, 89, 94, 101
Architects' Journal, The 36, 44, 85
Architectural Association 3, 50, 51, 58, 61, 63, 94, 115
Architectural Review, The 31, 73, 123, 129
Arlington Gallery 55
Art and Industry 99
Art Workers' Guild 44, 75, 106
Artifort of Holland 131
Arts Club 101, 109
Arts and Crafts 4, 25, 27-9, 36, 37, 44, 52, 55, 61, 103, 120, 122-3
Arup, Sir Ove 109
Ashbee, C R 28, 36, 50
Asplund, Gunnar 59
Attenborough, David 52
Attenborough, Professor 52
Attenborough, Richard 52

B

Bank of England 106
Barlow & Jones 87
Barlow, Sir Thomas 87
Barlow, Sir William 89
Barnsley, Ernest 27, 50
Barnsley, Sidney 27, 50
Barrie, J M 27
Barrington, Douglas 4, 31, 34, 90-1, 113
Bateman, C E 22
Bauhaus 51, 76, 106, 120
Baynes, Kate 26-7, 47, 49, 51, 58, 79, 106, 109, 120
Baynes, Ken 26-7, 49, 51, 109, 111, 120, 122
beds 25, 47

Bee, R H 51-2, 65, 67, 79, 89-90, 93
Beeching, Dr 111
Birmingham Post 38
Black, Misha 75
Board of Trade 83, 86-9, 98, 101
Booth, David 50
Bowes-Lyon, Elizabeth (later Queen Mother) 52
Bowes-Lyon, Lady Maud 52
Bowman's of Camden Town 93
Breuer, Marcel 76
British Rail 106
Broadway
    artistic and literary circle 27
    contracts division returns 115
    design team 94
    Duke of Edinburgh visits 113
    G R moves to 13-18
    G R returns after war 30
    intrigues architects 94
    mass production at 58
    materials skills 127
    and Murphy radio 58
    prestigious visitors and residents 52
    production for retail market 93
    retail showrooms 55
    influence on G R 9, 11
    Russell family as employer 67
    Toni Denning's arrival at 47
    visitors to 4
    war work at 90
    G R's working life 18, 22
Brown, Neil 131
Bryanston (school) 123
Bush Radio 63
Byng, Honourable John, *The Torrington Diaries* 15

C

Cabinet Maker, The 36
cabinet-makers 25, 33, 34, 36, 44, 51, 57, 59, 73,
cabinet, walnut 37
cabinets, radio 57-65, 119
Cadbury, William 65
calligraphy 26
Campden Guild 28
carpets and rugs 50, 67, 70, 73

Carter, Ron 129
Cassina of Italy 131
Casson, C R 63, 94
Casson, Hugh 75, 101
chairs, English oak 94
chairs, Thonet bentwood 73
Chinn, Trevor 79, 81, 93, 115, 119
Chipping Campden 4-5, 15, 49, 79, 105-6, 123
Churchill, Winston 83
Circular Saw, The 67, 73, 79, 115
Clinch, Edwin 85, 88
Coates, Wells 75
Compasso D'Oro design award 103
Conran, Sir Terence 5, 101, 123, 129
Corbusier, Le 51, 52
Cory, Edward 129, 131
Cotton Estate (Mile End, London) 11
Council of Industrial Design, The 38, 87-90, 98-105, 113, 120
Crafts Advisory Committee 120
Crafts Council, The 120
craftsmen 25, 27-8, 44, 119-20, 131
Cripps, Sir Stafford 88-9
Cromwell, Oliver 15
Cunard 27
cupboard, boot 38, 44
Cutler, H J 85, 87-8

D

Dalton, Hugh 83, 86
Darwin, Robin 98-9
Debenhams 55, 70
Denning, Toni *see* Russell, Toni
Desert Island Discs 109
Design 99, 123
design
    architectural influence on 50
    awards 103
    competition 129
    consultancy 103
    education 25, 98, 106, 123
    English 87
    garden 76
    industrial 50, 55, 57
    radio cabinets 59, 61
    new ideas in modern 50-1
    Scandinavian 76

Overleaf: the Gordon Russell
Furniture offices in Broadway